Endless Horizons

Journeys within a Journey

Poetry of

Brent Asay

1974–2016

ISBN 978-1-64349-032-8 (paperback)
ISBN 978-1-64349-033-5 (digital)

Christian Faith Publishing, Inc.
832 Park Avenue
Meadville, PA 16335
www.christianfaithpublishing.com

Printed in the United States of America

I dedicate this book of poetry to Carlos Egan Asay and Colleen Webb Asay, my loving, wonderful parents, whose lives of love, goodness, spiritual richness, and righteousness have in exceeding measure nurtured, enriched, and inspired me; who provided uniquely expansive and in-depth experiences for me in my growing-up years; and whose examples have instilled in me a love for reading and writing, and a passion for the written word's beauty and its power for enlightenment, self-enrichment, and good.

Contents

Part II

Part III

Prelude

Foreword

It is with great honor that I have been asked to write the foreword for *Endless Horizons: Journeys within a Journey,* a poetry anthology by Brent Asay.

Brent allowed me to read his poetry over the years as he began to assemble his anthology, and it provided a sweet oasis of aesthetic rejuvenation in a culture that increasingly embraces the crass and abrasive. I felt strongly that he should publish his poetry and make it available to a wider audience. His poetry is derived from the natural wonders of everyday life, and many of his poems are short stories told in verse. Brent's appreciation for the many pure and simple pleasures of life is infectious, feeding a spirit in need of the nourishment that only poetry can provide. Some of his poetry speaks of beauty, sometimes through pain but not with bitterness or cynicism. It is often pathos without despair. Brent dares to be intimate and personal— sometimes unapologetically sentimental—sculpting poetry from the raw materials of his own life experiences and creating literary murals that speak to those of sensitive spirit and artistically receptive hearts. I know Brent's poetry came to me at a time in my life when I needed poetry to soften the hard edges of life.

Richard LaJeunesse
Salt Lake City, Utah
May 2017

A Poet's Beginning

"Just what you want to be,
You will be in the end . . ."

Still plays a song a half-century old
Sure to resonate at least a half-century more;
First time hearing it on the radio
Touched off goose bumps to one's skin and soul,
Who with care touching needle to vinyl
Played it over and over, over and over.

"The trees are calling me now
Got to find out why . . ."

Hayward of poignant tune and lyrics, with deep mood guitar
In blend and flow with the melodic sounds of his voice
And the orchestra that was the Pinder-mastered mellotron,
Could not have known at all the transference between lands
Of the effects of his creation, like amplifier vibrations
In waves across the Atlantic to a teenage listener,
Of highest resonance to the teen's experience within
And from without, while submerged in intense
And contemplative identity and meaning search,
Craving, groping, for a saving outlet of expression.

"Just what I'm going through
They can't understand . . ."

His outlet of expression not in athletics found
Though pounded away his heart so wishing, so dreaming;
Beset with physical limitations, not blessed to run free,
But blessed to hear, and music hear—the wizardry
Of the Moody Blues sound, captivating fusion
Of music and poetry, cast mystical spell on him:
Their sounds channeled from vinyl or frequency
To the stereo speakers stationed in the teen's bedroom,
Like voices echoing from a golden dream or shining paradise.
Or like forces vibrating from out of a cave or distant galaxy,

Transferred creative energy and purpose
To the youngster's mind and soul,
Inspiring a poet he be along life's way
And spiriting the strokes of his poetic pen.

> *"I'm just beginning to see,*
> *Now I'm on my way . . ."* [1]

---

[1] Above italicized are selected lyrics from songs "Nights in White Satin" and "Tuesday Afternoon," composed by Justin Hayward of The Moody Blues.

PART I

Haiku

Poet with a pen
From depths of soul and life's cloth
Questing for the words.

Boyhood Yard

The mower marched through the grass
As my dad manning it cut rows neat and precise.
Through those rows I, an intent plodder,
In wee steps behind my Dad—
On he'd go, on I'd trail, but for break he'd call time
Smile at mom and glass of water.

A horseshoe pit at far end
Of the yard where grown-up men from the neighborhood
Picked teams, endeavored to ring up points.
Zestful in fun they'd contend
In competition engrossed, watchers amused stood,
Loud gusto outbursts all of good noise.

Over and over I tossed
A hard rubber ball against the side of the house.
If to height enough I lobbed it
A fly ball would carom off
And to the right spot I'd shuffle feet with mitt out.
The drill wouldn't end until summer quit.

At times the croquet mallets
Were swinging away, knocking the wooden, striped balls
To spots of gain, some to garden dirt;
Some with more knack and talent
By stroke of mallet blasted other balls to naught,
Their own through wickets to strike pole first.

Robust game of Steal-the-Flag
Played out its course through our yard and the other lawns
Of Wilford Avenue. To win out
Each team huddled and plan hatched,
Then sent out their fleetest to grab the flag, like hawks,
Rush back prize, uncaught, then "Winner" shout.

A backyard baseball diamond
At times, our hardball play fraught with stealing-home risk:
If the result a shattered window
Dad called out ultimatum,
Shooing us off and away with our ball, bats, and mitts
Elsewhere to bang line drives and flames throw.

But with bat in Dad's strong hands
Baseball buzz hovered in backyard's comfy confines
When Pepper he took us out to play.
Tall before us he would stand,
Flawlessly spotting our throws low, away, or high,
Swatting back grounders to our mitt chase.

Coaching words to us he'd shout
As my brothers and I the drill strove to master,
When Mom would call us into supper.
Once a Pittsburgh Pirate scout
Showed at his small-town home dangling him an offer,
Dad wowed us, passing food and butter.

Tomato fight erupted
On fall's tired garden as rotted tomatoes
Four brothers pelted at each other.
Into laughter we busted,
Our misfired volleys over the fence would go
Split-splash, squish, all gooey red clutter.

At backyard's west boundary
An outdoor basketball court crowned high with floodlights
Firm in place spun my world, stoked my dreams.
To that zone I would hurry
After school, to the hoop in the sky aim my sights
And launch shots tweaked just so for the breeze.

There I could be Maravich
As I dribbled and lofted up hoists, swish or bank
That alternated between misses,
And in it I was so fixed
Weather didn't faze me, plowing snow off, by rain
Undeterred, lost in sweat and wishes.

With friends sleeping out some nights
Encamped with our sleeping bags in the perfect spot,
Shunning tents for the preferred open.
With night air cooling more tight
I'd zip up my sleeping bag, maybe hear a frog,
Crickets, sounds by midnight spell chosen.

My folks kept a garden full
Of carrots, beets, melons, tomatoes, potatoes,
Squash, thriving by their faithful nurture.
Ripe and reaped, served at table,
The thanks given to God for manna, life, and home
Seemed a measure more lifting and pure.

2015

Ever Was That Way

When a questioning, identity-seeking teen
My parents one day reminisced to me
My very small boy tendency:
Quiet, keeping to myself, oft sitting alone,
Isolated deeply in thought and intensely focused,
In serious contemplation of something,
Nothing they could make out.
"What's he thinking?" they wondered.

Cannot remember those little boy thoughts,
But I ever was that way.

Scores of decades later
On a day warding off scorching sun
By much-welcome breezes
And a wrap of overcast overhead,
I was parked under shade of a park tree,
With windows rolled down for the cooling,
And there a crow bevy landed
On the grass under the verdant, full-leaved tree
Into the frame of my lowered side-view.

Six that I counted,
One over-animated and cawing loudly—
Wondered a bit at that, what its agenda exactly,
Maybe unsettled by the empty soda can inches away.
After short linger they're no more a minute
At that spot, for they in ragged formation scurrying

Crossed over the street to another grassy patch
And to the summer shade of another tree.
Then, so restless, they quickly fled from there
As though their beeping radar sensors discovered
Cooler and roomier shade lazing three trees away.

Contentedly secluded, transfixed by the scene, no deep
Riveting thoughts flew to mind immediately
Though some were in the wing and any second apt
To land upon the grass under the park tree
Company with the green, on-its-side Sprite can.

And now they are gathered.

Yes, I ever was that way.

2015

Every Day's Question

Well to ask what man lives for
That springs him from slumber, ties his laces
And spirits him out the door.

What of verity rules
His soul, what if fate has arisen too
And, vigilant for fools,

With an eye of dark regard
Lurks on the other side, there waiting?
Will passing man in life hard

To doom-filled fate plain give in
A slave to its unseen rallied forces
Or by inner anchor win?

2011

Michigan Journey

I.
To Michigan bound
Never wandered there,
Soon at the Great Lakes
I will pause and stare.

Wondering also
What else I will see,
Embarked from the West
Compass set northeast.

Some souvenirs of
Splendor will find way
Into my luggage
From a one-week stay?

II.
A lighthouse greeted
My ferry ride to
Mackinaw Island,
Seabirds gliding through.

Around the island
Tour by horse carriage
Past shops and town folk
Entranced by foliage.

Back in time, throngs walked,
Saw fort from the path
Winding down and steep
To town square's rich past.

III.
Off Traverse City
Afloat on the bay
The wet dark-blue silk
Made my kayak sway.

Oared my kayak round
To Lake Michigan
Straightaway I looked
Blue on blue to sun—

Waves as heartbeats
Of the flowing blue
Throbbed through to my heart,
Struck wonder anew.

Great Lakes like oceans
Grand ships traversed by,
Sails so majestic
I wished to still time.

2011

Wheelchair Imagination

I sit in a restless afternoon
Mesmerized by a chanted rhythm
Bouncing from across the street
Where a circle of pony-tailed girls
Rotates slowly their joy.
Leaping in and out of a rope
Their crescendos of laughter
Rise and circulate the air.

I follow the rope to hands wrist-twisting it up,
Forming up to an arch
Then curving down, skimming over bobbing heads,
Then scuffing the cracked gray sidewalk
Under frantic feet sprung up and suspended.

In my restless playful imagination
I zoom across the street
And swooping in and out of the rope
I jump not as high
But show myself as well, and as zestfully,
Playing with gravity, content with that.

The girls sprinkle out of the circle
And roam to another game
Chasing after each other, some hiding—
Then of a sudden from a vacant lot emerging
Hurdle sticker weeds and dirt-mixed debris
And traverse a series of mud puddles.

In the wake of their scampering
Follows my omnipresent imagination
Running with them,
Negotiating my own speed and distance
And even daring the wind
To race against me.
It wins the race but I'm content
With just having run.

1979

Up and Down Beale

Amid the skies of Memphis
One may be hearin' and feelin' the catchy
Captivatin' blues jammin' down below
And see at least one puffy resident cloud
In the shape of a guitar hoverin'.

Off to Beale Street go the two
To Saturday-night blues dancin',
Nothing better they'd rather do
On date night, nowhere else rather go
'Cause the blues they love,
And dancin's their thing too;
Nowhere better the blues than on Beale.

Blues flowin', blues aboundin', blues up and down Beale.

No matter which band playin',
Just so it's mostly genuine, unalloyed blues,
Old or new, up tempo, low tempo,
Original or cover, whether of Johnson or Hendrix
Of Clapton, Guy or Vaughn, or King's legend brand,
No matter to dancin' Joe and Jan,
They take it any way, relish it, move to it, moved by it,
They're one with it, twistin', shakin', foot-shufflin',
Stompin', arm-swingin', swayin', unwindin'
With movements so snappy and snazzy.

Guitarists of such skill and blues genius,
And some the greatest one's never heard of
Beyond Memphis and the Delta kingdom,
Who for the love of the blues on Beale stayin'
Or swarmin' there again for a festival in May
To play for the tourists, for the local regulars—
Yes, Beale's where they're belongin',
And there's way more to life than bread—
Indeed, they say, there's the blues, man!
And there's Beale!

Blues flowin', blues aboundin', blues up and down Beale.

Don't know for sure but would venture guess
Leon Russell has passed this way a time or two.
You can't go wrong on either side of Beale
Whichever blues club you're in mood to pick
For the band playin' in any of 'em
Plays the blues like knowin' the blues so well.
A keyboardist they call The Professor
Out from palms-laden California came
For a very, very long Memphis visit.
'Cause no better place the blues to play
Than Beale.

Asian girl in faded blue jeans fringed at bottom,
No more than nineteen or twenty,
Sportin' very long, dark silky hair
And stylin' in dark-blue canvas sneakers,
On bass is playin' for one of the bands.
She's in timin' solid with the drummer and lead,
Slightly her head a'bobbin' and knees a'bendin.'
At a moment or two you can catch her
Playin' with her eyes closed,
Floatin' and bein' soothed within,

So in tune with the blues, the band, and the scene
She could go on playin' all night.

Blues flowin', blues aboundin', blues up and down Beale.

A lady now rulin' the microphone
And the singin' voice she's renderin'
Recalls for a patron well-versed in rock
The same one he's heard over and over
On Pink Floyd's "Great Gig in the Sky."
She's singin' with pipes like Aretha's,
So beltin' and boomin' away
She can be heard way up the street,
There's a sense Beale Street is quakin'
Somethin' heavy on the Richter scale.
For the sake of those into full story tellin'
This diva of the blues featured tonight
Flew in from Shreveport long ago,
Ya see, there's no place like Beale for a gig
Singin' the blues.

A special guest took stage
Over at BB's place one night,
Like descended from that guitar-shaped cloud,
An old-timer flashin' a gapped-tooth smile,
A dear older friend of BB's
Whose old, long, and clever fingers were goin'
Head-spinnin', hummin' and flairin' on that guitar.
He was smilin' wider and brighter
And with high delight aglow, laughin' lightly
With each chord strummed, each string deftly plucked,
He was lovin' playin' the blues at BB's
On Beale.

Blues flowin', blues aboundin', blues up and down Beale.

Joe and Jan are still dancin' in the corner blues pub,
All the other listeners and dancers gone,
And the band just for the two
Is playin' one last blues number,
With a mouth organ burstin' out
Electrifyin' the air, as the guitars
Are glidin' and riff-cruisin', Joe and Jan
Dancin' a storm the last as at the first,
In the spirit and sway of the blues
Still baskin', movin', and thrillin'—
The thrill never stoppin' on Beale,
It just keeps a'rollin' and flowin'.

2014

The Brown Bakery Cart

The cart of fortune bread had been pulled on prosperous roads
Attracting a multitude of buyers who offered money
And a few zealous bargainers who crowded in, shouting
         and offering other means.
The seller of fortune bargained for death,
Forgetting money and betraying wisdom,
Exchanging bread too often for the drink of misery.

Breadboy, spitting in dust, dripping sweat,
Pulling the brown bakery cart against panting, stubborn wind,
Could have run away, left the cart, and joined the circus
But death claimed his father,
Left him with mother and sister
To take care of, yet see suffer.

The widow, black hairs now gray, fresh silkiness now coarse,
Worrying that Breadboy will be pulled by dreams
        of enchanting circus caravans—
Like husband was pulled in serfdom to drink—
Wonders who would sell brown bread, walk dusty-dusk earth,
And pull the bakery cart of brown.

Breadboy pulled here and there, bred to suffering,
Pulled by a gold world—a circus-carnival world,
Blown by want beyond suffering—beyond bakery carts—
Wonders too.

The widow dreams in silent panic
As she sees screaming beggars craving for crust,
   wine bottles lying in slimy brown gutters,
     and crying clowns scrounging for crumbs.
Breadboy asleep in the cold, blanket worn and thin,
Dreams too, sees mother slipping in mud
Pulling the cart of brown.

      1974

They Run

They run, and they run spiritedly.

The coppery, sleek-coated coltish one
Its mane brushed back by the wind
Slow trotting or at a gallop
In pastures fair and seasons young.

The fair-haired boy a fledgling toddler
Chasing after a flitting, teasing butterfly
Or a grass-stained backyard ball,
Or, if he dares, racing older brother.

The sandlot base runner like a golden burning dash—
A base path comet—his pals awed by his bat swing
And sprint around the diamond, witness with envy
Whoop and holler, watch his legend glow and flash.

They run, and they run free.

2012

You Skate for Me

I.

You trained,
You competed and entertained;
You struggled and sacrificed,
You sweated and paid a price—
All for success and victory.
But during all your ordeal
You were unaware
That all your dream, effort, and care
Were all for that one day—
A day you could not then see—
The day that you could skate for me.

II.

You could not see it then
And you did not know me then,
But if I could have been there—
And whether I had been a stranger, lover, or friend—
From front row and rink-side
You, I would have watched and enjoyed
And richly admired, while you skated so poised;
I would have been basking in
The marvel and in the fascination
That was purely and only you.

III.

I would have fastened like a magnet
To the sight of you, and lost myself
In your melodic motion:
My heart riding along on your rhythmic glide,
And my eyes an absorbing, focused spotlight
On your beauty on ice
That I would have thought my prize.

IV.

If I could have been there rink-side,
Either alone or watching with others,
I would have watched you endlessly
And thrilled to your every movement.
For you I would have clapped, cheered
And willed you strength and precision.
My heart would have ached
Should you by chance have fallen.
Yes, I would even have cried
If, by some fluke or mistake,
Defeat had been your fate.

V.

But now you skate for me, today,
Rusty and older you are, you say,
But in twisting unfurl still you shine
A sparkling jewel in spin and twirl.
Your spin, form, and glide
Cause me wonder and pride
And, most of all, captivation—
That will no doubt last—
For your glittering beauty on ice
Remaining from the past.
You create for me clear vision
Of how beautiful you were then,

How truly majestic on ice
You must have been.

VI.

As you skate in these later years
Out on a park's winter rink-side
I, lone spectator,
See surviving as I stare
Your splendor of yesteryear—
Seeing more than just a glimpse
Of a skating goddess
In an ice-crystal palace.

VII.

Although not skating together
We somehow are one:
One skating so gracefully
And one watching, hypnotized—
Intertwined and bonded
The moment we share.
While you skate
A rush of joy I feel,
Sheer pure rapture
That leaves me fulfilled,
Fulfilled by you—
Fulfillment better than victory,
Treasure more than all medals gold,
Yes, truly you skate for me.

1993

Sharing the Hills

Simply there for the deer, their known
Hills of home. Rock, streams, brush, and rays
There to feed, scamper, sleep, and roam.
We know there few men make a home
But some often go there to play.

Not to deny man the honor
Of building a home on the hills,
It's his if he has the dollars
But it's known not just by scholars
That hills are home to the deer still.

Live side-by-side with them, that's fine,
Splendid there your hill-home but know
If munching your tulips and vine
Are they, it's nonsense if you whine
For perhaps they've no place to go.

2011

Somewhere Between

My being
Somewhere between.

I'm between home and work now
On I-15 South, past the refineries.

A three-quarter moon a mere pale shadow
                                    of itself
Hangs in the grayish blue of the
Upstart dawn's might flexing
Somewhere between March and spring.

Just a day ago thought I witnessed
In mid-March winter's last white fall
But perhaps would get played on me, on you,
The same heartless trick in February when winter's
Shackles and icy tentacles lifted into the atmosphere, and in the
Vacancy sprung two sunny days that warmed us body and soul,
But next day we saw, we so sharply felt, the cruelty of
The warmth doused like a helpless lit candle by the storm winds
As the shackles shoved down, the freezing tentacles thrust down,
The snow and ice and a colder us restoring
Back between stark winter and spring.

Well, weather meanderings enough
So to the radio I turn with a sigh.
Too quickly, enough news of economic ills
And the world's tragedy, despair, and hatred-burn.

Another sigh along
I give the sports pundits a chance.
But this morning they just prattle on so,
They're saying the same things over,
Bombarding me with clichés mercilessly
In a sport's different season is all,
Or not talking sports,

So now I've got Knopfler
Playing maestro on the guitar, a song
Of his going to be a free man.
He keeps playing, song now
Of his awesome darling pretty.
My heart
Somewhere between divorce and love.
At least one day closer may be getting closer?

I'm closer to work now.
My car's gone the same path so many
Times before it's hypnotized, it could
Drive itself to where I'm going.
I've almost stopped sighing and yawning
A half mile from work,
Be there very soon
Traffic and self willing.

Somewhere between March and spring,
Somewhere between the dying moon
                    and infant morning's sun
                                    Am I.

                    2011

At the Light

Intersection light fierce-red, car panting at a pause,
There I sit, for the switch to green waiting
Behind the wheel, and about ten cars back,
And out the rolled-down window could
Without strenuous socket-straining reach
Extend my left arm like a yardstick
To a hopeful one whom I see up-close
Just in front of me to my left, entirely harmless
Appearing, and beggar's desperate condition
Betraying, the light glaring fiery red.
He waits to see me act before he makes full approach
As he's got eyes on other lined-up cars
All at the same time, watchful as an adroit spy.

Us both inside a random moment spun out from
This earth's and life's enigmatic whirling and delivery
Of people and place, time and circumstance,
That puts me at a traffic stop and him close by
Hoping I have some random change
Stashed somewhere in my pocket or car
That I can spare and pass over kindly, quickly.

He appears bedraggled and beat up by life
In drab, worn blue jeans and sullied shirt,
Being beaten by late afternoon gusts of warm wind,
Bearing crude square of a small cardboard sign
Whereon inscribed, "Need two dollars for a soda,"
And this jars my mind to my present money affairs

As I think of my shoe-string budget
Between paydays, and just a few days back
Groceries I purchased for sixteen dollars
To fill fridge and cupboards for a week.

He's master of the subtle trick
Intently noticing cars yet appearing not
To eye them so keen, his dark sunglasses complicit,
Fully suiting his purpose as if befitting
A beggar's code of decorum and class and scruple
To annoy less, to more likely coax favor.
Craving, aching, for a fountain in the desert
In his quiet beseeching he wishes from me
A dangled-out, cupped hand with quarters inside
Or even just one (a dollar bill could blow away)
And would that of any amount
Increase his daily supply, or be it total?
I so wonder as the light fixates on red.

Only an infinitesimal scrap or crumb he wants
Of my more abundant purse it seems he signifies
As I vacillate, tussle with the inevitable question
Do I give to him or not? Suddenly forced upon me
The quick decipher whether need or con
Is exhibited before me, tugging at me.
He's unaware I'm searching for change in my pocket
As I twist in my leather seat to reach therein
And then to pull out my wallet and peek inside,
Though still unresolved to impart what I can give.

Any more worthy his cause, any purer his heart—
Be he worthy or pure in the first place—
If humbly yearning he implores me, "Alms for the poor,
Alms for the poor?" Cries of olden, eerie chord,
Of despairing, rending tune that hauntingly arrested
The air then faded on those ancient passing winds.

To green the light switches, abruptly my thinking shifts
As the slightest cranny of time remains wherein still
I can give, for I wait for the cars in front
To roll on forward and clear first—
Then, finally resolved, quickly
I fumble for pennies in a dashboard cubbyhole
For neither my pockets nor wallet store a coin.
To the beggar the benefit of the doubt I dispense
Since God only who can judge claims us both His
Like the wind, benign or rough, regards us the same.

Sadly, I fussed and wavered too much, too long hesitated,
To the resolve too late, no pennies snatched up in time,
For I had to move on, and now the cars further behind await
Their turn, and the beggar for them sets just right his sign
And waits, their mercy to beg, their consciences to try.
Right there, steady, he'll continue his back-and-forth
As intermittent gusts swirl and buffet him.
And drivers worn from the day, eager for home, who chance
To notice, might care to evaluate him, his cause consider.

2013

Working Class Woes

The shiny rope to pay dirt heaven
Is always beyond your sweaty reach,
Your journey is pointed to the coast
But you'll never find the golden beach.
You struggle, you search, you yearn
But nothing much seems to count
Of what you battle to earn.
You are running but running in place,
Surely, you are just taking up space.

No one really seems to hear your voice
And you then begin to wonder
For all this did I ever have a choice?
But on you hope, on you crawl,
You hope to rise, but there you fall.
Even if somehow, for a dizzying moment,
You grabbed hold of that rope,
Surely someone would cut it
Putting you on the ground to grope.

You can look all you want to me
For what I can muster of sympathy,
For I row upstream, swim against the tide
As you do—I too am simply resigned

To this life's calamity, this life's fate
That we neither planned nor could instigate—
But could be therapeutic if we commiserate.

1995
Dedicated to Alexander Solzhenitsyn

Wake-Up Call

The Athletics up two games to none
Determined to win, redeem themselves,
To win big, to squash and oust the stun
And cruel pain of one year before
When odds-makers had them winning all.
Their fate spelled though by a Dodger ace
Named Hershiser and Gibson-stroked ball
Over the right-field wall, making hero
Of him injured walking lame and goat
Of then game's great closer Eckersley.
The upset was sprung, the As had choked
And the sports universe in awe quaked.

Hung heavy the anticipation
Over the park known as Candlestick
Of the Giants ending the frustration
Of twenty-four years of title drought.
Though stalwarts like Mays and McCovey
Long graced the field, mesmerized the fans
And gave them reward for their money,
Now the team's time to rally and win
Though two games down to a star roster
Of McGwire, Canseco, and Stewart
And other stand-out performers,
Now the Classic on the G's home turf.

Bay Area brim with fall magic
So thick in the air it could be struck,

Popping against a bat, wood smashing,
Nothing more perfect for the Pastime
The sports pages and magazines read,
Two teams apart by a baseball's throw
In the game's highest drama, so said
Pundits and those peddling story line,
But just one could see the scare looming
Of Ruthian proportions at least,
Frightful beyond a fastball zooming
From Bob Gibson on the mound glaring.

A scientist to something dire
Pointed days before, and cop horses
Were one minute in panic's mire
Before came the heave rolling, roaring.
Foe greater than demons of the past
Or long time's chain of futility
Struck blow: San Andreas' heavy bat
Took brute rip at the World Series.
The stadium, the field, and concrete
And steel forced to jolt for mere seconds
That seemed longer, sharp froze the heartbeat,
All afraid of the Big Final Out.

Turned the A's mission and the Giants' dream
To other aim, stuck in not a game,
Their hearts taken in cruelest siege
And by gross uncertainty assailed
Whether underneath in the clubhouse
Or in harassed stroll through the tunnel,
Snapped to feeling like a crawling mouse,
Deeply engaged in pre-doom warmups;
On the field were shocked players already,
Dazed, searching to see if loved ones were
In rocked lower stands holding steady,
Life-long dream of sudden a nightmare.

Blockbuster contracts, security
For their lives and for their cherished ones
Rendered now doubtful as thread flimsy,
So thin against the pulsating fear.
Goliaths of baseball felled to ground
Level and common with fawning fans,
No batter up, no pitcher on mound
To stir fans' frenzied marvel, instead
Dark-bent, gloomy questions abounded:
Where to take shelter, where to be safe?
Seemed no one for this had accounted.
Safe in the stands or out on the field?

Rings and trophies far from hearts beset
By fear of what could swift happen next,
How the right-field foul pole swayed left!
Rumblings over? Please, please be over!
Instead of the joyful yelps and cries
Of elation from crunch-time home runs
Belted skyward, or dazzling the eyes
A double play so magically
Turned quick, heads of fans put to spinning,
Or a player for ball-snag the fence climbed,
This about the losing and winning
That comes from dying or surviving.

Such the all-star this nature's mauler
It fast-balled asterisk to Game Three.
Waxed so somber the game's booth callers,
Felt the Blimp the upward rumbling waves.
Those who missed the Series that fall night
Anxious the score to find and digest
Found no relief from the grind of life
Opening the paper next morning,
Denied reading brilliant box score stats,
First seeing front page dominated

By seismological facts and graphs
And that which dodged the obit pages.
Amazing the poise of fans and players
With fans still entering, some leaving,
By fans or teams no mad foolish errors:
Alarmed but in collective control.

The earthquake's inception on prime time
Reminding all who were there, who watched,
Life trumps sport, against raw released might
Man's helpless, no doubt, like dust, like ants:
Death's closer in the bullpen grinning
And scheming to throw curves and change-ups,
Waiting, warming up in late inning
To flame out lives, to reap his triumphs—
Grand Slam lesson to the sports-consumed,
To our sports-opiated masses.
No game played that night, Series resumed
Ten days hence, Game dusted itself off.

For the record, for the game's annals,
The As won two more at Candlestick
And if scribes above were impaneled
To take any note or care a whit:
In Loma Prieta's dread shadow
Baseball's best were crowned planet champs
Yet subdued flicker the victors' glow,
Greater cheers for Life's crunch-time rally.

2014

Kayaking Mystic River

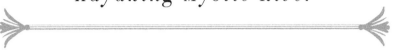

I'm stroll-kayaking the fairway mile
Of Connecticut's inviting Mystic River
Bordered by boats and ships
And some other vessel kinds
On the water business side,
And posh dazzling summer abodes
On the other side lazing
And the bridge siren tolerating.
Startled riverbank dog barks reply,
By its too-short nap irked.
Ship of yore sailing masts
Usher my way into timelessness.
There in the splendid middle
Yonder lighthouse my vigilant guardian
Detects me closer to bridge.
My carefree course I oar
To a slow, cruise rhythm,
Passing boat repairer on dock
Whose notice I surprisingly elude
As I continue leisurely along.
Beyond point of bridge reached
My gaze in outward drift
Spots where the river merges
Into the soaring blue vastness
Where for a short moment
Hypnotized I take to kayaking
By my mind's paddling oars
The dreamy upper cerulean spheres.

Sunny companions to my meandering,
Seagull trio sweeping by lighthouse
Glides me the way back
To my vessel of solitude
One with Mystic River's wonders.
Wonder what the Algonquin tribes
Observed in their kayaks homeward
To villages beyond the thickets.

2014

Inheritance of Cards

Baseball treasure cards showcasing
A '49 Ted Williams, Triple Crown Ted
Who batted in 159 Red Sox runs that season,
And a '51 rookie Willie Mays, the Say-Hey Kid,
He of basket-catch and other spellbinding
Fielding exploits, with power bat to match—
A father lovingly entrusted to his son,
About three hundred cards in all, a museum in shoeboxes,
Half a factory of bubble gum chewed and gone.
Baseball-possessed boy razor-focused
Studied back-of-card player stats like batter
Intensifying eye on pitcher's windup
As if valuable information and insights to absorb,
The homework he must finish so his
Baseball smarts surpass those of his buddies.

His Dad's prized the Son added with curator care
To his own proud, sterling collection:
He managed to barter a '71 Nolan Ryan,
All-time no-hitter hurler
And dubbed the Nolan Ryan Express, for
A '59 Mickey "The Mick" Mantle, The Commerce Comet
(More into pitchers than batters the other card merchant).
And in another marvelous, glowing trade
A '69 Lou "Base Burglar" Brock and a '72 Pete "Charlie
Hustle" Rose for a '73 Tom "Terrific Tom" Seaver
And a '75 Nolan Ryan. And Dad's eyebrows
Raised at that, surmising the Rose card

Not so valuable, likely yields less dividend,
For Rose's betting scandal rocked baseball
And all of its die-hard believers, no healing in the wake.

Son tore up and trashed cards
Of Mark McGwire, Barry Bonds, and Sammy Sosa,
No honored place for them in gilded shoebox
For all the damage and disgrace
They upon baseball heaped.
His '96 Derek "Mr. November" Jeter card rising
And rising in value by the year, and Son was close
To tagging "Yogi" Berra but couldn't give up
His '70 Reggie "Mr. October" Jackson.
Not just trade value mattering, for some players
More than others won over his fascination.

One time he was amazed, almost paralyzed
By disbelief, his '67 Bob Gibson
And '68 Denny McLain (thirty-one games
Pitched and won in a single season)
Could not spring him a '65 Sandy Koufax
The Man of the Golden Arm.
Undoubtedly out of the question
The likes of the Babe, Pee Wee Reese,
Bob Feller, Gil Hodges, and Mel Ott.
His dad never got remotely close
To close to them.

Son swears on his '66 Don "Big D" Drysdale
Never to give up, never to part with
His '69 Roberto "The Great One" Clemente,
Pirates legend arguably the ballpark's best ever,
A relief effort torchbearer at thirty-eight
Dying in cargo plane tragedy
As life-saving and hope-giving supplies
For Managua earthquake survivors were reduced

To the floating wreckage and rubble
Of a doomed flying mission.

His card of all cards, Joe "Joltin" Dimaggio,
He's lacking but on bold quest to obtain
And more hopeful than a year ago because now
He knows a friend who knows a relative
Who knows a friend who knows someone
(Of the old school, wheeling and dealing online
Son rules out of field of play, banished
To the obscure bleachers and as lowly esteemed
As all the spilled crackerjacks crunched underfoot).

Son is very well pleased with his Vida Blue
Orel "Bulldog" Hershiser, Kirk "Gibby" Gibson,
"Hammerin" Hank Aaron, Johnny "Hands" Bench,
George "Lou" Brett, Ron "Louisiana Lightning" Guidry,
Rollie "Mr. Mustache" Fingers, Lou "Sweet "Lou"
Piniella, Jim "Kitty" Kaat, Greg "Mad Dog" Maddux,
Mike "Iron Mike" Schmidt, Frank "Robby" Robinson,
Joe "Gentleman Joe" Rudi, Jim "Catfish" Hunter,
Ozzie "The Wizard" Smith, Brooks "The Human
Vacuum Cleaner" Robinson . . . .

If he could swing it somehow would he
Sacrifice a '67 Carl "The Yaz" Yazstremski,
A '69 Willie "Pops" Stargell, a '72 Dick "Richie"
Allen, a '64 Juan "Dominican Dandy" Marichal
(He of the windup high leg kick)
And a '77 Steve "Lefty" Carlton (the curveball
Rembrandt) for a Joltin' Joe of any year?

So the collection business trundles along
And Son wonders when his trading ends
To whom will he pass the treasure?
Probably resort to coin toss
And the one of his two sons who loses
Will by his cherished sports car
Be compensated sufficiently?

2016

Whispers in the Attic

Where the roof leaks
And wets the wood
Of bug-whittled holes,
Petrifying the dingy and stale air,
The past creaky and dusty
Whispers in the attic quietly
And subtly, acting
As the unheard of our lives
Shelved, boxed, piled, and some locked—
Stifled by the noises of the now.

Maybe just momentarily forgotten
And dormant
Hiding from us, where we hid it,
Waiting for us to recover it
At rare moments we escape
The exigency of life.

We throw not everything away,
Saving the souvenirs of our lives
With promise to ourselves
Rich meaning they possess.
The meaning fades away
Until we awaken
From the coma of time and routine
To fathom it.

Dreading the chore
Of digging away the dust
And tidying the attic
We climb the creaky stairs
Up to the cramped, lonely attic
And enter with heads stooped,
Fumbling for the light switch—
We hurry to get done
And get out.

In our fumbling and fuss
We bump fragile boxes,
Contents spilling out
And splattering the floor.

Then looking we're caught in the state
Of the obscured and now-dormant present
As pieces of the past
We hold up to our dry eyes
Like mirrors to our faces—
The past reflected in us
As we're reflected in it.

1981

The Bingo Club

Half past six to the sharp every other Wednesday night
For bingo night, the social room booked,
And Cindy once again there, setting up tables and chairs precisely so,
Ready to greet the Bingo players arriving from their apartments.
Most as well-dressed as any other time of the week
Except maybe Sunday—but dress no object
For this all about the company, fun, and gab
Though for vigorous play, strictly by the rules, as if great sums of cash
Were at stake, released by rich palms, upon a casino table lying.

As Cindy ornaments the prize table with fancy unwrinkled cloth
They all begin popping in and settling into their accustomed spots
Seated and scooting up to the hard-plastic table sides.
They're a varied sort of folk, at times a lively, entertaining bunch,
Now with eyes fixed on the game boards set before them,
Tossing light chat around—weather was fine the other day
And my how the cost of prescriptions has crept upward—
As now Cindy stands, positioned table-close, and revs things up,
Booming out the letter-number combinations,
Just popping them out in playful gusto, in high tempo cadence,
Almost one could picture her a veteran auctioneer on the county fair
    circuit.

"B10" barked out, as if by a zesty, energetic drill sergeant,
That invigorates and spotlights Tom, a first-timer.
Some of his fellow Bingo players might be surprised, if they knew,
His younger version played three years of minor league ball
In the Midwest, couldn't hit the long ball so didn't make it to the Bigs

But some he saw pass through that world of dreams and unknowns
On way to the Majors, no one whose name ever lit up the sports page
But they were great players just the same in his expert estimation.
A contact hitter predominantly, one home run to his name
He parlayed thanks to his lightning speed, an inside-the-park gem.
If asked he'd speak fondly, wistfully, of those magical afternoons
On the sunny diamond, and tell you he misses the smell of ballpark
    grass
And with a laugh tell of the time a fuming coach sprung out of the
    dugout
And cussed him out for watching a stray pigeon roam the outfield.
Lucky for Tom the batter struck out! He dodged a fine but after the
    game
Still ran laps to the playful taunting and ribbing of his teammates.

There just to the right of Cindy, sits Beverly, about whom
The other Bingo players would not know unless she told them
She's lately been agonizing over her daughter Bethany
Whom she split with over religion years back and so long ago
It might as well be a century; longingly Beverly still hoping for
And awaiting a call or card from Bethany during the upcoming
    holidays,
But too acutely knows most likely neither will come—she's afraid
The acerbic feelings and alienation are too entrenched, and already
Four phone calls she's made, leaving messages, all unanswered—
Frightfully worried each time calling, fretting how Bethany
Would react picking up, or might message acridly receive,
With matters left sadder and worse for the effort.
Coasts apart and the passage of time yield
No healing power, at least in her case, Beverly laments.
So hard for her to stifle the memory of that awful day
The arguing and shouting with Bethany spun out of control.
Beverly believes in faith so she keeps praying, tearfully reaching
And beseeching though pained her numerous prayers unanswered
Like her phone calls—she despairs, tempted to just give up
On heaven's powers, but knowing Bethany shuns prayer

One of them should still be praying, Beverly figures, as she's
Leaning more to believe in God than not
And steeled and brave enough to exert faith and wrestle disbelief.
Somehow she finds some sanctuary in Bingo night too.
She confided in Cindy once, a palliative talk, a few Bingo nights ago.

Jolly and jovial Harold chuckles to himself his letter and number
Has yet to be called, but just glad to be there at Bingo, so tired
Of watching so much lame television, and it would be mighty right
If his sweetheart in heaven called him up, her way,
A little more than a year ago since sweet Suzie passed.
So long ago returning home from Korea, elatedly into her arms
With joyful tears, he thought that his first stroll in heaven.
There were so many close calls that could have put him there
Before his sweetheart he felt had an eerie courtship with death,
At least flirted with it so often, in and out of foxhole or bunker
Or taking ground, bullets whizzing past, fellow soldiers who got hit
Laid out in agony, conditions so wretched, some he helped bandage up,
He thinks he's already done sufficient time and burn in hell,
Could never bring himself to watch MASH.
He'd swear to anyone the 62 letters Suzie sent him saved him
Like a wellspring of God's repeated good graces of protection
Pouring forth upon him from the heavens above.

The Andersons, Scott and Lisa, weeks ago came beaming to Bingo
And still are beaming, all smiles and radiant faces, eyes aglow,
For their 60 wedding anniversary they had just celebrated
With their 6 children, 35 grandchildren and 10 great-grandchildren,
Feeling so fulfilled by their family and so blessed they've had each other.
They hold hands still and seem just as in love now
As they were when poor, love-rich newlyweds, touched by
The favor and smiles of Cupid showering upon them.
To the future they look ahead brightly, to eternal bliss together.
Scott uses a cane because of chronic hip problems
But sometimes he'll lose the cane to walk unaided
And if walking too long causes him struggle

Lisa gives him her shoulder, and happily they'll walk along.
And that's how they came to Bingo tonight, together laughing,
And Cupid still smiling.

Lane sits at the end of one of the long tables
With the hint of an air of superiority and sophistication
As if perched at the head of the board room, dressed dapper,
Conducting business in his successful banker days.
Apartment living is starting to nettle his nerves, especially so
Now he's coping with the news of contractors two more months
Delayed in the construction of his retirement abode.
To Bingo he usually comes grousing about money.
He first struck the others as a whining, sour kind of a man
But from getting to know him a little they've found
He has a wry sense of humor that sometimes entertains.
Answering to the playful shout of "G13" from bubbly Cindy
He wishes they really were playing for money.
His morning's bad start got exacerbated when he learned
The Dow had dropped 200 points, and he's getting better
With it but still is pained from the nasty memory
Of the thousands he lost in the economic downturn a few years back.
That memory revived within the regions of his brain and soul
Almost a year later on a bleak wintry evening, on the telephone,
When Blake, his youngest son, with a wife and four kids, sobbingly
Reported he had just lost his job, and Lane one to take care of his own
Financially supported them until Blake after long last secured a job.
He thinks a crime the state of the economy, weakening and sliding,
Seeing three grandchildren graduated from college with high honors
In a long, endless search trying to land gainful jobs
Having to live at home with their parents, Lane to himself bemoans.

Bingo's a momentary rescue from boring solitude for laid-back Joe
Who suddenly squirms in his chair from a light jolt
When "N68" Cindy calls forth—
Not because he had a match
But because letter N recalls for him Nam

And 68, the year he finished his soldier tour of duty
And returned home to the States to loathing
And stigma rather than welcome from fellow citizens
That made him feel every bit a war victim.
Unknowingly Cindy had struck raw nerve in him—
A subtle yet potent sensation apt to catalyze
The flooding of memories through his nerve channels
But by steely refocus upon Bingo summoned up
He managed to defuse the heavy impulses
That had tried to compel his vivid recollection
Of Agent Orange, Charlie, the Tet Offensive,
Journalists and photographers scurrying about
In the midst of the searing, mad action in search
Of the next famous prize-winning story or photo,
How he managed to stay away from the drugs,
How close buddies with wives back home vanished
To the villages of beyond, his resentment of Hanoi Jane.
If he was to share: Even in the midst
Of all the gory scenes and ghastly sensations,
All the grisly horrors of war, he felt he was fighting for
His country: Proud of his service then, and even prouder now,
True patriot then, even greater patriot now.
And if he was to tell:
He and his surviving motorcyclist veteran buddies,
Nearly a dozen service honors among them, about a week ago
Cycled their cause up State Street to State Capitol,
The country's flag tethered to each shiny-silvered Harley, and waving,
For wounded vets and their families, raising money for them.
With gushing pride he'd boast they raised north of $8,000.

After several rounds Bingo now over,
Effervescent Cindy calls the game to completion.
They all turn in game boards, slide chairs in,
Someone asks about tomorrow's weather
And one announces the launch soon of a book club.
"Why did rent go up on us good, long-time tenants?

I'd swear we're being nickel and dimed," Clarence observed
Out loud, to no one in particular.
Cindy reminds Judy to bring prizes next time
And urges them all to come back in two weeks.
After counting 18 who played that night to her patented rhythm
And as the mostly grateful, goodwill goodbyes fade out
Cindy turns lights off, closes door behind her.
To her apartment returned, on calendar pressed by magnet
To the refrigerator she marks X, noting for herself
Glowingly proud, the 22nd time her charm dazzled at Bingo.

2016

Unwritten Epitaph

The kneeling youth gently wipes the dust
Off the tombstone front
And reads only an engraved name.
Weeds act as relics of the funeral flowers
That once laid in bunches on the grave,
Later torn apart so chaotically
And swept away by the winter chill wind.

The youth recalls the snowfall in mellow cadence
On the still winter day as peaceful
As the life of the one who laid asleep,
So naturally tranquil the scene seemed.
He remembers the crying of those who mourned,
How too grievous it was
That one of their most loved was gone.

"Gone but so alive"
The feeling echoed in the youth's heart
"Gone home to the God of love."
His hope for reunion strengthens
From memory of the poignant moment—
"I too will return," he preciously realizes,
Expression of that hope
Places flower upon the grave.

Time passing, wind furls the lone flower,
Entwines it in a stray weed
And diffuses dirt in loose gather

About the tombstone of no words final
On the life of a man filled with love—
The grave a mockery of the man
Whose life of love and goodness deserved
The exalting riches of eternity.

1979
Dedicated to Aaron Elias "Lyle" Asay
My grandfather

Late Autumn Reflection

The sky a blue never before my eyes have beheld,
A different reflection of color, ray, and angle
To my vision, to all my senses; my mind differentiates
and my heart absorbs the meaning.
The color is different from what I saw
In younger gaze to sky, like my sense of self and space
That once was my minuteness felt standing before a building
Overwhelmingly big, imposing, and daunting then
That now seems smaller now I'm taller, older, counting.
The feelings from what now I see different so
Compared to way back then, and more varied,
The oft-heard songs of yore now touching and echoing
within me, in newer dimensions,
And the wind I feel differently, to an inner pang
As drifting season-aged leaves playfully brush past me,
Precious seconds on autumn's clock ticking away.

2012

Song Heard in Winter

Song heard in winter,
Notes suspended and frozen in air
We can see our breath.
Tiny echoes falling and turning to ice
Or mixing with fog or following footprint trail
To snow bank by paralyzed stream.
No walking stick can pierce that iron ice.

Song heard in winter,
To the sound some march along, some trudge,
Some walk lamely, some with trepidation.
Oak limbs droop fragile and lower for the cold,
Replying sad song sounds within
The chambers of the lonely heart,
Soul pained by the words and melody.

Song heard in winter,
Tune that taps chord
Of the enchanted season, the enraptured harpist.
Long look back on a year gone by,
And the pensive thin-coated looking ahead
Shudder amid fright and dark uncertainty.
The ruthless wind taunts, crying derisively,
Incessantly, against the heavy, melancholic heart.

Song heard in winter,
The serene hush or holy interlude:
Silence resonates for some.

Some with hearth that's warming
Hear refrains of cheerfulness
As festive color and renewals harmonize,
And in too-few places the ring of church bells
Thaws some of our icy suffering
And unclasps some of our freezing chains.

Song heard in winter,
Tells of death's certain and unfailing part,
The leaves red and gold afire long vanished—
But though the lonely cry
And their small, brittle candles light no more,
Flow hymns of angels to wise men
And Star shines in silent rhythm
To the joyous chorus of hallelujah.
Stars now as then offer radiance,
Constancy and promise to all men,
Songs now as then—resonating prayers
For light and love, warmth and peace.

2016

PART II

Haiku

Sometimes poems cheery
Sometimes fires of the soul
And oft-times a mirror.

Plea for Your Love

Saw a moment for me so, so true
When I turned about and there was you,
The soft wind wafting by also knew
Something as sweet as the spring dawn dew.

Could I be lucky, play right the odds
Or work some magic to sway the gods
To win your heart, your love receive?
Grand dream or plan, or fool's belief?

I'm getting older, time moves swiftly
My window for love closing quickly
You know I've ever been a true friend,
My heart and soul with you to the end.

Oh! Please! Lovely One—come, come my way
Please take the time and feel what I say:
Love you I have, I will, and I do
If only you'd come near, love me too.

2011

Critics of Vicious Prey

Some critics after vulgar deed done, after vicious and successful smear
Of a person, of an idea, thought or principle, or of something produced,
To the increased misunderstanding and confusion of others, exacerbating
their ignorance,
Get handsomely paid for their craft of deceit, the spoils they salivate
to procure.
(Could they have made a living doing anything else? Producing anything?)

And they, driven by more than envy that they the idea did not conceive,
Are still not quite fully satisfied, still ferocious,
Now like slavering vultures circling above, in macabre ritual just waiting
While eyeing the carcasses lying freshly dead and horridly below,
Embolden and armor themselves in perniciousness to snipe and savage
The creator and messengers of the sound, intellectual and fool-
ish-proof position.
For they want to convince that those persons and their existences,
Out-of-date, unpopular, have no place, right, or validity—
Not only never to be heard or believed but subjected to
Measures of being shut out, voices muffled out,
And their characters massacred, reputations mutilated, and names
maligned.

So bold are these critics, some say, and so persuasive are they,
So sophisticated and newsworthy in the words they formulate and spin
they must be right
And in the name of politics or comedy, it's all fair game, so they're
justified too.

But perhaps a critic more heedful to the call of logic and reason, if
    privately asked,
And after lamenting some critics tend to be believed more being
    more visible—
More often on the mainstream camera and mike dignified—
Will call these snipers experts in deception, in dressing their manne-
    quins of thought
In the finest color and fabric, in garish appeal, faking us into believing
Something significant of compelling depth is harbored therein,

Or will call them critics of vicious prey, skilled in damning common sense
And principle which, to give credit to, or the merest consideration to,
Diminishes them, for whom the facts are so many pesky flies to be
    swatted away,
Who, if others are raised up justly and meritoriously, and rightly praised,
Cannot selflessly join in the rightful deference for the attention is
    not to them
Making them feel less and to fear—so teamed with corrupt media for
    fullest effect of smears and propaganda,
They work and rework their designs for revenge, and attack
And reattack, and their calculation that powers their assaults against
    truth,
And this wretched place which their sorry competence and warped
    consciences occupy,
Horrifyingly devoid of tiniest shred of shamefulness or pause.

2012

Necessary Nuisance

The same obnoxious, bold freight truck
That powering its massive hunk
Across a warehouse district street
In thick of morning's rushing beat
Provokes honks from cars oncoming
And curses from drivers cussing,
Carries goods to destinations
These drivers go on occasion
To buy life's necessities
Or joy-sustaining luxuries.

This sometime road-rage catalyst
That seems on street least politest
And tending to heat people's blood
With no merchant name emblazoned
On belly, cargo hid inside,
Hogging the street with its full might,
To numerous merchants carries
Product loads that of kind vary,
Maybe medical equipment
Or substance for making cement,
Or the latest in furniture
Or moving with care light fixtures—
All over the truck leaves its marks
In enterprise transporting parts—
Or maybe carries much lumber,
Or to make wheels, pierce-proof rubber.

School buses are also known
To clog lanes for cause we uphold,
They equally can so annoy.
But must light minds, girl and boy.

2015

Thoughts of You as Miles Roll by

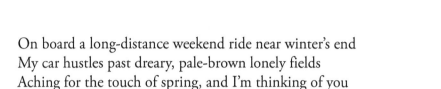

On board a long-distance weekend ride near winter's end
My car hustles past dreary, pale-brown lonely fields
Aching for the touch of spring, and I'm thinking of you
Only of you while listening to music on a magic machine play—a guitar
Masterfully plays while in duet plays that something in my heart for you.

Chorus harmonies mixed with crescendo waves lofted by instruments
Catapult me up out of my car, and for minutes, I'm afloat on wings. Sadly,
Song ends, I'm no longer soaring, just staring into the sky now.
Abruptly, in the winter-weary sky two spry winged friends meet my view.
From a power line they twirl off each other into an extended spinning-out
Then between flight and hover alternate, perhaps sensing spring is nigh
Inspires their flapping zigzag dance.
I think of another movement as special as dance and flying
Just as exquisite to me when your shoulder you offer me
So I can walk strong and uphill ascend.

Like that timeless song that never plays on the radio enough, that I
    can hear
Over and over again, is your voice striking an enchanting chord
    within me.
I've tried turning from you like dialing to the music of another radio
    channel
But the echo of you always returns within me
And my mind can't hold back the thoughts of you.
I now hear a piano playing in a song, giving off pleasant, tranquil
    sounds—
Could I compose a song that could be played on the keys of your heart?

My soul's deepest desires seem to hang on a dream and chase a mirage
But they are daily breathing strong, staying inspired, and are now
    expressed
Over the miles unto you in not quite the right words, perfect words
    elusive,
But the words with feeling flame in peak iridescence, like candle-
    chandeliers
By the thousands set in rainbow-esque suspension above
Forevermore by magenta sunsets kiss-lit, and somewhere there
My heart's expressions blaze as sweet radiant song unto you.

2012

Politics and Lies

God will judge
With justice and mercy, knowing all, the entirety
Of our words and works, the substance of our characters
Whether within or outside the political world.

God will not pardon judgment
Even if it was the press, persuasion, and play of politics
That caused lies and deceit and other forms of corruption
To glitter forth specious to win minds and hearts
To achieve the desired ends of some conniving men.
For the source and fountain of falsehood God knows.
No declared untruths to be exempted by His law
By a waiver here, or a waiver there, or rammed through
In aberrant use of an option called reconciliation.
The source of all lies and deception He knows—
That slippery serpent with uncoiled tongue
Far and wide stretched and meandering
In laughing but truncated season, cunningly devising
And spewing its vile venom throughout the halls
And chambers of power, and poisoning the organs of media.
Someday at last, during the Final Resolution, the Omnipotent Almighty
Arraigns and stabs the spineless viper.

God will not blink with sympathy
Even if the label "free speech" or "campaign rhetoric" adorns the lie,
The lie no less because a political one,
No less scandalous because of origins and aims political,
Even if all the fabrications of the political planet

And all the concealing and scams
And all the chicanery and dodges
Are all fashionable and cleverly clothed
In the trending narrative, spin, or talking points,
For very long ago God exposed and rebuked
Satan, the Author of all Lies.

Man conceiving and promoting such things
And the poll majority in blind lock-step applause
Even by the grand sweep and glory of popularity
Produce no swaying justification for God
For He, the Father of Truth and Light
By thundered fire strokes into mountain stone
Commanded, "Thou Shalt Not Lie."

2015

Feather Surf

Off-white, velvety feather in knapweed
Marooned, motionless, and forlornly trapped
As though fated to endless misery
Fortuitously by a breeze is freed
And lofted upward, high and aflutter,
Then by faint windbreak it's jolted a ways
And now surfing a current of charmed air
As long as the dreamy ride can sustain—
There at stream's end a moment suspended.
Midst this magic voyage to wondrous regions
Nature's whim orders the wind's cessation,
So the feather now meanders lower
Its course altered so it's hang-gliding down
As passing butterfly swerves to miss it.

Still descending, upon earth soon to land,
Now it's two feet or so above ground
Hopefully not to alight and be stuck
But in non-encumbrance freely stationed
So next time the wind decides to dance
It vaults up to sway as destined waltzing partner
To glide up high into the upper spheres
And float long like a helium balloon.
It's eager for the next breathtaking surf
To ride it out long, in gusto, renewed.

2013

The Alley Cats

A menacing and brash motley bunch, prowl the alley cats
In scraggly formation on a midnight foray:
Their picked tandem atop the high and splintery wooden fence
One in front, one in the rearguard, as if tower watchers.
They're all in brawny and bold pursuit, scavenging, exploring
Under a hot august moon in the sultry tar black.

Reputed as hopelessly wild and a loitering, miscreant lot
They're expert at scheming, looking to push further out
Their territory, claim new ground, discover new resources.
The nemesis of backyards where tamer, pampered cats
Subsist and watch time, alley cats known to pounce on a few
Of the dainty ones who stray a little too far, and that fatal,
By the border of the alley, and whose caretakers
Take to mourning after receiving the ghastly news.

Alley cats bear their share: Unruly teens bent on curing
Their summer boredom one night came after them
Toting BB guns, one not so much boredom-bit
As swearing revenge for the awful wounding of his sister's
                                    fond and fair dainty one.
During scarce seasons, the demise of some by starvation
Sorely lamented, no more deeply grieved than that doomed night
A horrific screech and shrieking horn they heard
And caught scent of iron-hard rubber scorching asphalt
                                    from frenzied wheel-spin,
Terrified at view of one of theirs on the road sprawled out

Writing in agony and fires of pain, a bloody, convulsing
                                        blob in the sticky oven air,
Chest heaving, and suddenly its sharp, spine-jarring scream
                                        speared the night.
Two by teeth-hook into its trampled, filthy coat gained
Traction, and choppily pulled, and with some other paws
Pushing scooted its crumpled mass off the cruel road
To the gravel strip, then toward a farewell resting spot
In amicable brush, whimpering as they mourned.

They a resilient bunch on the morrow roused themselves
                        at the sun's stirring, the advent of dawn,
Shaking off the cobwebs of slumber, mindless of
The feline carnage of the night before, their odyssey
                                        of survival resumed,
And though not wearing dignified tags they live the honor
Of their reputation they're not always seen but always there
In ghostly shadows, in endless, tormenting mischief.
No morning cat-napping this crew, for they're about
The obnoxious business of toppling over street-lining
Smudged-silver metal trashcans, giving off a clanging din.
They clamber about and pick over what spilled out
Like shoppers in produce handling and appraising
Bananas and other fruits for mushy spots and bruises.
They're grating the nerves of on-looking residents,
Worse for some for hearing cat claws the surface of metal
Scratching, worse than a violin squeaking too long.
Generously the alley cats leave scattered, loose spillage
For the refuse collector, their garbage man friend,
Who later-arriving blisteringly curses their existence.

Under the ebony sky so thickly and stiflingly dark
Spread again, the alley cat on lookout, atop patrolling
As the others sleep and dream (in some sphere,
                                        they must dream)
Resting for forays on the morrow, halts its back-and-forth

Of a sudden, and trains a sustained gaze into the only light,
The half moon's eerie misty-yellow glow reflected
In the mysterious glinting of its cavernous eyes—as though
From a glaring cosmic truth drawing power.

And transfixed still, stares past fear, pulsates, and a chord
Purrs that like a brooding whisper permeates the night
With coarse accompaniment by the annoying drone
                    of the irrepressibly chirping crickets—

So the night throbs and cries, and omens, for the alley cats.

2012

Tribute and Farewell to Robin

I.

Day after the genius humor hero—
Indubitably you—moved on
Where I live the sky rough and dark
In pain and protest cried long
In pounding, mournful sheets of rain,
And many hearts quaked with grief
In reeling, sorrowful anguish
Tailing our initial disbelief.

Oh, that a powerful malevolent one
Working evil and fear upon mankind
Would pass from this place, leave us
Be and of a securer collective mind
Than one great and good as you who gave
So many, so many moments to laugh
Should have to go, dimming the golden rays
You had bestowed us by your presence and craft.

II.

The rainstorm has stopped, dark day
And mourning over, some sadness still lingers
As our hearts begin to heal,
Your legacy pausing to remember.
Our fortune your works and wonders preserved,
Treasured are my memories of you, Robin,
How you made me soaring laugh, in stitches.
I believe you believed in a heaven

And now watch from afar wanting us to celebrate
Your endless merry fest of laughing fun.
So atop a desk I stand, and standing persist,
Thanking and honoring you, Captain Robin.

2014
Dedicated to Robin Williams

The Shell Reaper

The sun hazed over
By a shifting cloud cover
While at water's edge
A man stooped over.
"You are looking for what?"
I curiously asked.
And the man on beach raised
Eyes to me, out of his trance,
And uttered, "Shells," as through
His hands and fingers weathered
He sifted sand, cupped the find
In palm and worth measured.

"Once a beach harvest
Of shells aplenty,
Now like a gold mine
Fast going empty:
As more seekers of
Shore magic there are
I've had to wander
To beaches so far."
A thread of woe
In these words he said,
In this plight of scarceness
His soul has bled.

Beneath sand and receding
Roiled water the shells lurk
But sift more and more he must
To gain the elusive perk.
He moves on, so
Methodically slow
Tracing the water's edge,
Eyes on what's below
As he seeks out another
Spot more fertile.
Slightly he stumbles as his
Foot glances a tiny turtle
But still staying low
With eyes of precision
He sees, suddenly, a speck
In the soaked sand glisten!

Sweet discovery! He reaches down
With hand and raises the prize,
Holding it precious in his right palm.
His soul exults as in joy he cries!
He's now the rich lord
Over this treasure spot!
But will harvest or want
Be tomorrow his lot?

2010

Out of Route

Saturday traveler winding off the on-ramp, quickly
Finds he is out of route in territory unfamiliar
Lost on a northeasterly path
While a crow never out-of-route follows
Overhead, on its path of untold miles.
An accidental brief journey embarked under
New vistas of sky, and new lolling landscapes wherein
                                 his metal horse to run
In a brilliant bursting at noon of mid-May sun.
The traveler in a warp, in a ball cap and
Shades, watches the path closely
                 to the first exit.

Prominently first into his highway view a sad
Dingy old car of train-rail rust color, dull silver
Splotches on its side, window cracked as though
A bleached spider web, crystallized, is fossilized in it—
Metal carcass at the margin of a barren
                      plough-waiting field, stranded,
Kept company by a mile marker of the blandest gray
                            fifteen yards away.
The relic is out of route, unclaimed, waiting for a tow truck
                            to play its pallbearer
To convey it as is, no cosmetic formaldehyde fix, un-coffined,
To the bone yard lorded over by a restless wicked bully dog,
Like a cemetery but no epitaphs there
Like one the traveler once saw, its entrance ground staked

By a dirt-plastered yet decipherable sign, slanting slightly
                                        discernibly left
Proclaiming, "Recyclable Parts for Sale."

Thinking of parts and where at last they rest
                    or find restoration,
The traveler wonders as he cruises, as the odometer
Clicks a digit, would he donate his organs and tissue
To the theories and test tubes of science if a disease
                                    that would cure.
Like a liquid of particles sunk to bottom and diluted
                                        more at top
Now shaken well to its sound and finest equilibrium,
The traveler's bleary consciousness is jolted to the day's
Necessity by the sign just up ahead. Two miles to
The county line road exit, he's got to wheel around, get back
                                to the route of destination.
Next curving into his view
A speed limit sign blaring seventy-five
Maximum, forty-five minimum. His mind-whirl
From the cold, commanding numbers austere as stone
Spins out the thought very close, to the bone clear,
                                and wistful
That age forty-five, he blew past a good time ago—
A historical fact like the in-the-way, slower car he just passed—
And maybe, just maybe, if fate smiles upon him
He will live to at least seventy-five years old.
To himself says aloud, robustly confident
As if so expressing convinced, reached him
Inner-deepest, "I feel younger than forty-five,"
As he guns his Solara to eighty-five. Buoyant
In speed, he overtakes an SUV and Porsche, like he's
Racing at Indy, and he's to that exit head-twirling swift.
Off-ramp he slows, then horseshoe-shaping to
                        the other side

He's en route southwesterly, to where he was
                                    pre-off route
As a winged blur seemingly from under the front left
Bumper bursts into a millisecond's view, then across
                                    the highway darts.

A few minutes by, looking off left
The traveler sees the abandoned rusty car
                                    still has not moved,
An arc of crows flies over it oblivious

And nowhere a tow truck.

And thinks
Could be its driver is somewhere, coping
                                    out of route.

2011

New Star, New Paradise

Your appearance on a late May evening
Like a goddess out of a dream, or out of a mural painting
By a master versed in picturesque beauty all of its ways,
Was secret delight and fortune to this poet—
A new star of promise illuminating his night-sky
Spinning the motions of his mind and soul,
So he penned:

"The magic of your golden hair I'd love
To touch and draw close to my face,
Drown my senses in its scent
And take my time playing strands
Of your luxurious hair in my hands
And even try to weave them into a braid.
Your soft and delicate voice suffused with
Warmth plays so captivating gentle
On the light summer air sounds like
Notes of a melody played in love's heaven.
I wish I could hold your hand
And its softness raise to my lips to kiss.
I'd love to caress you, kiss your velvet lips, so I could
Closer draw to the essence of your beauty, of you.
Your name that rhymes with daisy—
Which can only be one golden—
Only right I should be picking untold dozens
Out of a lush meadow for your favorite vase.
So loved how at "good night" you said my name

I'll name that new star, this new paradise
After Kaylee the Goddess."

("News flash to Venus: Your oft-adored station and prestige
In the galaxy, and your reputation being of all loveliest
Have just been replaced, happy to report.")

As they say, as reality reminds,
Timing is everything.
This poet can't alter or influence time
But oh, that he could!
And, oh well, as the days and nights go
Certainly he can
Think, feel, and believe
And wish like any irrational fool can.
This poet's spaces of emotion
That these wishes inspired by you permeate
Are so real, and though out of time with Time
He'll awake to them in the morning
And in them bask the daylong.

2014

The Scarecrow

Bankers turned beggars
Stare at the scarecrow
Of straw and feathers,
Pain it cannot know.

The harvest hero
Once got much credit
For scaring the crow,
The town—he fed it.

Great harvest of maize
For once God didn't bring,
For scarecrow what praise
For the town to sing?

Once an idle god
Vainly praised by man
Now to man a fraud
With feet of tin can.

Farmer of crop woe
And banker bowed low
Gaze at the scarecrow,
Hunger it can't know.

Stands painlessly still
A tattered scarecrow.
With powerless will
Death does vain man know.

1978

To an Oriental Goddess
(On Valentine's Day)

Elegant character strokes sculpt your name
                                    to mean *beauty*
But in any language
There are no words or characters right enough
Or in supply enough,
And all the flowers in a teeming garden or floral shop
Are not enough
To describe how beautiful you are
                being so, so beautiful to me.

Your beautiful being
Adorns my face with a smile, shines a golden light
                                            on my soul,
Your laughter releases an exhilarating rush
                throughout my innermost chambers.

My indescribable feelings kindled
                                by your beauty
Here laid before you to outlast
                        all of time's flowers
Flow deeper than the rich roots
From which rise any lily or rose.

2012

Cries of Winter

Mad, boisterous snowdrifts hurtle into the bleak night
By the cruel whim of winter winds, the leaden features
Of a seething, bared-fang wolf with doleful eyes
Holding graphic sway in the disfigured and savage sky.
The orchards are being mercilessly whipped:
In unremitting fright boughs crackle, kindred branches
Viciously torn off shoot to the ice-scorched earth
Of the exceedingly long, excruciating path for those
Dragging themselves through freezing tempest homeward.
Cries for warmth, compass, and safety are drowned out
In the din of the engulfing, ferocious fury:
"Where is the Rescuer? Where the Sun?"
Cry the terrified, helpless voices
Of the beaten-to-numbness, bone-weary inhabitants.

2014

The Gardener's Gaze

Like an explorer after far and wide odyssey
Ecstatic over crystalline gems lying
In an ancient treasure-womb he discovered first,
The gardener, soil-crusted spade in hand,
To the soil squats down, arm reaches down,
And like drawing up from a well
Scoops up mahogany, mineral-packed earth
Close to his face brings it, and by its
Touch of mulch and bark-like scent sweetly transfixed
Ascends in tingling rebirth
To climates of golden-most splendor glistening
And silver-most dew fall sparkling.

Eyes glistening like from a vision, the moist
Rich soil he rubs between his thumb and fingers
Then plunges hand with tool into the richness,
Descending reaches the ideal shallow depth,
By the tape of his forefinger length gauging,
And with meticulous finesse lays in tiniest bed
Amber seed of purest wholeness and potential,
Then with sculptor-care and spade flashing sun-tint
Spreads and pats into place prayer-laced layer—
Blanket resistant to the harmful or the pest—
Over the earthy embryonic gem.

By act of sowing quickened the gardener
Into bluest, cloudless sky and effulgent sun looks up
With pale, out-stretched arms and beaming, praising eyes.

A skylark idles in aura of morning's glow
Several feet away upon a small
Mossy mound of rocks, altar-like,
Serenading too, when of a sudden it masterly
Summons the air and wings upward and away,
Its echoes from bright notes sung spiraling up
And in light-flowing course merging with
The waves of the gardener's heavenward gaze.

2014

Seven Days to File

"7 Days to File" warned the sign
By a tax shop gopher swung around
And he a splash in a clown's costume
Under the frowning, gray-dripping sky
Of an April Monday afternoon.

Dreary taxpayer made to account,
I pause to take jaundiced, scathing stock
Of those to whom I must answer true
But creeping-up deadline can't discount
Despite my plans or citizen view.

Flashing their high titles, versed in con,
They to me merchants in corruption
They've too long been on a par with clowns
For their deadlines they put off way long
Only to drop on us sad account.

Once a young lad learning history
Was taught tea got poured into darkness
By citizens blasted with taxes,
Now we too suffer in misery
When cold and ruthless taxes slam us.

Such shame our stewards play rotten their part.
We are made to balance our ledgers,
They're busy with other things and plots

And concoct their scheming to such art
Public tours of the White House they stop.

This still America-?-work do I
Some will against arrogant power:
A form snapped from perforated line
If I have signed and postmarked in time
Pardons and frees me till October.

Because meager sum I'll receive back
I've determined this much for myself:
That if they're in no hurry to act
I'll follow suit no thanking, then ask
Do they and I worship the same flag?

2013

Oasis in Silicon Valley

There amid Silicon Valley's slick
Hi-tech spread and conglomeration,
Its starry heights of human advancement,
I was with a Filipino Goddess who showed me about
And showed me acre after acre after acre
Of rich-yellow dandelions near her home,

And took me on a garden tour:

Through high wooden gate swung open
Into a Bay Area yard I entered,
Then embarking on a circling path became
Instantly immersed in an extraordinary scene
Of a treasure of flowers and small trees and climbing plants
That I felt the warm aura of the orchid in late winter—
Like a stirring and soaring vision,
A breathtaking embroidery of stem, vine, and leaf I saw
Throughout, with orchids in state of eminence over all
                    Mirroring the beauty of the Goddess.

A nursery architectress, a seamstress of nature,
She envisions the garden's destiny
Imagines all its wonders, and touched within
                    Designs and dresses it:
Where one can slowly stroll and tarry, forget life's burdens
Battles or bumps, and in the ordained season be renewed
Plucking a cherry, apple, or blood orange from a tree.
The maroon-tinted orchids so very pleasant to the sight

While nectarines there so very sweet to the taste
Surely alighted winged guests do in ecstasy bask
In matchless fortune of seeing the garden, singing joyously,
While unseen angels awestruck and breathless
Witness in hushed pause, then in serene quiet celebration
Meditate upon all the beauty and truth there
For anywhere pure beauty and glorious truth is
                                        Is heaven.

I beheld the Filipino Goddess in a pocket of sunlight
That imparted glow on light-rose azaleas in the garden-paradise.
Moving through alternating blocks of topaz light
And mellow shadow of the late morn, still gazing around,
I could spot and name a lily but few of the surrounding flowers
And leaning over, picking one of white petals, perhaps a daisy,
Breathed in its freshness, its effervescent and renewing scent.
She spoke passionately of such wonders, in revelation
Of something quite quintessentially mystical,
And how sometimes she talks to them in low, soft tone,
                                a nurturing whisper,
How only in vesper silence bloom some flowers,
Nearly convincing me her garden holds the kernel secrets
Of the universe, and of her soul, while even more I'm warmed
                        by the zestful rays of her creations.

On sky-voyage departing Silicon Valley,
Barely after lift-off, I peered out the window
Through opening in a wispy cloud to the valley below
And in reflection of the garden and its Goddess-creator
Mused upon the magnolias in purplish-pink
To bloom three weeks later—what hue, beauty and spirit
                        and fulfillment they would blend
With the other radiant and enriching forces
                                Of the oasis.

2013

Thoughts on Love
(In the Lack Thereof)

Man can't lone and without the woman be
God hath said, and if to be now
Or after this life the bliss achieved
Most want it in this life somehow.

At times bitter-sweetly can't help but think
Love so right failed to me intend,
How so deep into pain the heart can sink
When love seems close but is not meant.

When you least expect it, occur love will
So don't go work or search in haste
For love, as some sages say is the deal.
What's spent on date could be a waste.

A path the weak of heart should not dare trod,
To go that way can bring out fear.
For the deep rewarding life—one to laud
It prized—he'd best be sound and clear.

Some brave would traverse wide freezing rivers
For love, face blizzard or sand storm
Or tho online oft snubbed be no quitter.
But smarter to bide time the more?

True love never had by some who're wedded.
Money, pride, or selfish of heart
May intrude and be embedded.
For some all love or have no part.

Better to be lonely in single state
Than in marital condition—
The one a vastly better, saner fate,
Best wise against flawed decision.

Love one just knows, or is work, or is both?
More to die for than to live for
Or of each an equal part must take hold?
True love found the soul needs no more.

2013

Sufficient and More

The curtain on fall's panorama not quite
                              all the way drawn—
True, the harvests are well past
And the leaves mostly have peeled off the helpless trees
                    which mostly stand barren, colorless now
After bullied by swirling breezes and northerly gusts
        exposing bulky nests in forked-branch crevices lodged.
Nearly all swept away
Like the birds gathered instinctively
        in synchronized hordes, compassing
Then streaming the flyways arced through the dome
                          to go colonize for a season
                          warmer skies and ground.

But the sun pours forth exuberantly
        in late November, a Saturday afternoon
        upon a small clearing creek-close
        patches of grayish-yellow brush,
And the wanderer poking hard ground not yet winter austere
        with reddish-brown walking stick, drawn five more steps in
Sees crimson wild berries, some in clusters, cling to shoots
              of fragile twigs protruding from the creek bank,
              gently swaying, dangling.

Not all cold, not all withered,
Not all bye and beyond.

Nature's nurturing answer, merciful, to the autumn mostly passed,
A tranquil, mellow respite before the storms,
Today, the sun predominates, reigns
        warms the sparrow that hovers, teetering from a fence-post.
The creek bed mostly ice-layered
        but from late-morning thaw
Melts into mini-streams that trickle
        roughly parallel with the edges of
        a jagged procession of thin ice plates.

Tree-top branches from the south creek side bow across
        to touch elevated bare branches lurching over
        from the creek bank north,
Rendition of a harmony of nature.

Yes, not all faded, not all far-flung.

There is light, there is warmth, sufficient and more
                        this afternoon, this season.

2011

November 16, 2013

Winter is dark, so blustery and cold
Rain pelts down, to snow will turn
In grimmer assault, besieging this Saturday night.
Into asphalt puddles the chilling pour
Of half-rain and half-snow settles, then by morning
Solid into sleek and impish black ice.

Winter, that Siberian icicle that never melts,
That serpentine draft that slinks under the door
And winds up into my shelter interior,
And sinister, scheming, seeps through
The once-thought impregnable walls and window edges.

Winter come again too quickly, so abruptly and rudely,
And I'm shivering in a fog of loneliness.
To escape it, or at least ward it off,
Over my body will pull my puffy bed covers,
Lay my head on the soft cotton pillow, comforted by
Increasing warmth—cozy, safe warmth passing
Over me, through me, all around me,
Easing my being to sleep and dreams
Soothing my heart to tranquil, protected hibernation—
Waiting for the dawn
And warm hopes of the morrow to break.

PART III

Haiku

Spring-begotten dreams
In beds of winter's gray snow
Longing for sunshine.

Monarch and Songbird

The sunrise is over.

The butterfly in winter barely past
Morning young, unfolds
Its velvety wings, springs
Off the sodden wild grass,
Stretches forth a Monarch
Mighty and majestic
Soaring off.

The morning is brighter.

A songbird, nearby perched, arouses
And ebulliently trills.
Its music echoes
In vibration upward, softly,
Like cotton touching to cotton
                    (if could be seen)
Rising to the tree's highest echelons.

It is noon, blue so clear.

The Monarch and songbird
Over meadows, ponds, and knolls
            just past winter's sting, now warming,
Radiate their freshening presence
And ardent spirits, defying
What was winter's bitter hold

As the sky has mostly shed
Its ugly, gray winter garb,

Their spring dawn rites rendered.

2011

Daylight Savings

The clock last night sprung one hour ahead,
This morning found myself so long dreaming in bed.
Time to bolt out of winter's protracted slumber
And blaze forth as the sun, soul unencumbered,
Release power full, unleash all my vital forces,
Exert my energies like freed, sprinting horses,
Sidle along Main Street, cycling my three-wheeled vehicle
By hands and arms, striving for freedom's pinnacle.

2012

Morning Cat

Cat on windowsill
Purrs and slowly yawns
And in sun lies still
At peace with day that dawns—

Warms fur against window
And with a glance entreats my view:
What it sees and senses I cannot know
But I'm moved, born into day that's new.

The cat and I somehow relate
In a comforting, mystical way.
In moment's pause I serenely contemplate
The morning cat that welcomes me to the day.

1992

The Farmer Poet

He's a farmer and a poet.
He's tiller of acre and word
Always with eye and heart for seed-fertile ground.
Of vital vigor to his soul-blood
Are the sun, earth, water, and sky.

Under the rising sun
He stirs, wakes, and warms.
He dons apparel, eats day's first meal
      and to his deities prays.
Then to the fields of his daily labor
        beats a swift path.

He eyes lush emerald mountains
     under the brilliant sun
By which he day-long measures distance and land
Like he heeds the zenith star's compass
To fix his evening orientations.
By day he plows a field, and as the ground into
        furrow after furrow forms
A line or two he crafts.

Behind those mountain peaks in majestic array
That he counts like syllables in a line
Shimmers the turquoise sea that carries
      tiny fisherman boats
       leeward and about,

Whose wind-play currents recall the annual
                              delivery by sea
Of bundles of bountiful harvest sprung forth
From his labor—Destined for far ports
              And to feed hungry sailors
                      Out upon the blue.

He's reaper of harvest supernal and galore
                    and of thoughts sunny and noble,
The one in autumn only, the other a daily yield.
Give goodly syrup and spice
The sun, earth, water, and sky
To the life-affirming, ever-flowing nectar
Of his verse.

In procession of early dusk, day's work done
He strikes for home in pleasant stride.
First, short visit he pays to his fond village
To fulfill last obligation of his day
Which a privilege, highest honor, he deems.

Master of the Haiku
He with engraving tool, with artful and dexterous hand
Carves three lines into soft, compliant wood
              of seventeen syllables in all
For imparting the day's wisdom he harvested:
To an upright bamboo pole by the village well
He posts the engraved Haiku in offering
To the village officials, peasants, and rare visitor.

They gather round.
They read, absorb, nod heads in agreement
              and marvel with pride.
They're glowingly pleased, more enlightened, they know
That poetry's not treasure and domain only
Of lords and their courtiers in royal mansions

Or their aristocratic friends, as just one more
              of their cultural prizes and novelties—
Haiku neither cryptic code nor exquisite art
For nobles only to divine
In their courtly estates, transcendent surroundings
                    and conceited states of mind.

He's a farmer and a poet.
For the villagers, he's hero more
Than the samurai or the emperor afar off.
Now leaving the village for home
He smiles as he passes, and bows to his peasant friends.
In the peace and lamp of sunset
They bow lower to him.

2014

Never so Alive

Into the garden of the living
And the brilliant meadow of glowed awakening
You have brought me,
For like the in-season flourishing in color
And unfurled form, scintillating and fresh
To the senses, a stirring, buoyant rush throughout,
So alive never I have been.

Never so alive!

In heart-to-heart flow with you
To the sunny paradise of happiness
You have taken me
And there lit my soul with a flame
I never thought could glow
Acquaintances on my daily rounds
With little effort noticing, and without hesitation,
Observe to me I look so happy,
Tickled they've discovered something new about me,
Seeing a joy in my eyes also shining upon my face
Perhaps they never thought possible,
And they can only wonder the reason.
It's a treasured knowledge and sublimest feeling
Because of you I have felt
And which to the heavens I could sing,
So happy never I have been.

Never so alive and happy!

Out upon the waves of serenity,
Upon an infinite feeling of comfort and pleasant calm
You have set me sailing, peacefully afloat,
Where I feel safe from any treacherous wave
And securely warm against any wicked season or storm
For such joy and fulfilling completeness
Never I have felt.

Never so warm and complete.

Seems in the far beyond of the universe divine
In that uncharted, mysterious vastness
The stars of destiny the guardians of love have aligned
In perfect symmetry meant only for us
Under our Maker's sweet, loving graces,
For such blessing never I have known.

Never so alive and happy and blessed!

2015

Five-Dollar Single

"Belt a clean base hit
And sprint safe to first,
No fluke off a mitt
Just a clear-through burst,
Son, and I'll give you
Five dollars," dad said
As the sky shined blue,
Dreams by the sun bred.

No time did lad waste
When he to the plate
Strode, some cash to make.
The ball saw its fate
When he swung his bat
Aiming for fortune.
His teammates roared, "Pat!"
Watching the ball run
Fast, sharp on the ground,
Blast up the middle
Past the pitcher's mound
Lined straight, no wiggle.

Past second ball streaked
Into center field,
First base met his cleats
And he was fulfilled:
The umpire yelled
"Safe!" that the crowd heard,

To first Pat had sailed.
Back to first he curved
And so buoyed, triumphed
He to dad did shout
"You owe me five bucks!"
To strike out all doubt.

The cash tactic worked
For pitches galore
He smacked afterward,
And each run he scored
Each hit that he banged
Each out he fielded
Victory's bell rang
And magic yielded—
Treasures for the boy
That throbbed his heart,
Nor trophy nor toy
But sport's joy the spark!

2011

Skipped Rock

Palm-sized rock, saucer-shaped, and side-arm tossed
Instantly pierces and carefree skitters along
The sun-sparkled bluish-green surface
That pre-toss was absolutely calm, immaculately still.
The flung rock, a speck in the blue the rock-skipper
                                   squints to see,

Abruptly ends its forward penetrating glide
And starts to sink down now
With faint ripple outward from sinking point
That vanishes quickly from his eagle-eyed view.
He yearns he could follow its path downward
On this morning of awakening and innocence
And would dive, hold breath and watch underwater
If only warmer the water and he clad right.

The rock somewhere in the water's depth lies buried
Deposited in the large pond's quarry bottom
Of a mother lode of rocks of wide assortment
And of origins traceable to the bank and surrounding earth,
Now lying below vulnerable to crust fragility and shift
                            and the flows of time.
Higher, the luminous surface, fresh like the morning,
Intersects with the sky-blue at the horizon,
He discovers viewing the still opposite bank,
Glancing over the submerged pondweed, closer-in,
                           tickling the surface.
Then his tilted upward glance finds the sun

In its morning innocence shedding warmth and light
Upon and around the bed of water, and on him standing,
Nestled in nature's calm and contentment.

Another sidelong glance spots
Close to foot of west bank willow tree
Sun-splashed spatterdocks mirrored
In aqua surface restored tranquil,
And drifts to the sense and wonder
Of the lone figure upon the bank
The fragrance from a light and soothing breeze
As it passes over the large pond water
And gently up to the tall wild grass
Encircling and brushing softly
His riveted being upon the bank, massaging
And scenting his eyes-closed, serene meditation.

2012

Strawberry Gold

Partaking a strawberry bulb-shaped
Crimson and luscious rushed a blend
Richly throughout the buds of my taste
Of sweet pulp and juice of blessed stem.

And upon my second perked tasting
Even keener the permeation;
Inner links clicking, integrating,
My soul won nostalgic occasion:

Walking with Dad across weed-quilt field
Lateral the irrigation course
To where water destined for ground tilled
From out of chained gate came tumbling forth

(Once the sluice gate Dad raised securely),
Then hurried through the cement channel
Unto patch of planted strawberries,
Leading trek back over loose gravel.

Precious water from ditch reached garden
Minutes before our backyard return
Then glided a controlled direction
Of runlets as stray twigs afloat curved.

Vigilant, Dad had shovel ready
For chance of breakage in earthen maze,

To ensure the waters ran steady
So the roots drank even in their take.

Strawberry row after gardened row
Thrived whole at the water's arrival
Climaxing their Eden-yearn to grow
As gold rays kissed soaked copper soil.

Considers the sunny red moment
That it only to a treasured day
Belonged, and reveals lesson salient:
All gold to a boy of Fifty-Eight.

2016

Visit with Emily

Time passes like rushing waters for you, Emily,
Or in pacific, gentler flow of perpetual contentment?
Like a sprint the past several years have swept by me.
I'm at loss how old I've become so soon, too soon,
In this earthly time and already six years
Since you my first granddaughter
After being light and life and wonderful promise
In the sanctuary of your mother's womb
(For a long but too-short time)
Were called back by our Eternal Maker.

Emily, so much closer to comprehending
The mysteries of Time and God, you than I
But no question for me, no doubt,
My measure of faith in God is nothing
And my ardent belief in Heaven-after vain
If no more beyond a wish, dream, or fantasy
Can I feel and know you are somewhere
A six-year-old playing, some joyous, splendorous place
Where purity and innocence abound and reign
Where angels your playmates frolic with you
In hopscotch, or skipping rope, or turning cartwheels,
Or through aureate meadows meandering without care;
Where I can see you exhilarated and smiling
With your mother's smile as you run down rainbows,
Your long hair like your mother Raquel's aglow,
By genial breeze your past-shoulder smooth strands
Floating in comfy and free Elysian sail.

Death to my believing love is timeless,
Tragic to my faith, and utter despair of my soul
If I allow my heart and mind to succumb
To the dark and frightful contemplation
My transition will be marked only for
Prevailing conditions to bury me in nothingness
That seeing you, or any loved one, is impossible—
Or, continuing on, awakening into the next existence,
No occasion to see you flows my way,
But my faith overcomes and girds me stronger, convinced
No bonds more lasting and true than those of love,
To prevail all throughout the flow of Time
And graveside I stand here speaking to you
Feeling so certain you hear me.

Emily, you must know the overwhelming overflowing
Of the love your mother possesses in her heart
                                        and treasures for you
Equal to the love I'm sure you have for her.
A child's pain and suffering—the loving parent's
Agony and trial of mind and soul,
And Raquel's I so sharply felt after your passing
As she mourned and wept and groped for answers.
The passage of time has healed her heart, matured
                        her wisdom and perspective,
And now, certain as I know that I stand here
                              reaching to you
I know Raquel's love for you ever grows
In yearning reaches out to you and sustains
In fervent blossom her hope of one irradiant day
You and she in sweetest, joyful embrace reuniting.

2015

Kiera, Ethereal

Barely of one-inch circumference
My six-month old granddaughter's supple hand
Daintily she curls to softly hook on my finger
In trusting earnest grip, and Kiera sustaining the hold
Buoys my heart with joyous, ineffable peace
Telling me the paradise from whence she has come,
By her innocence and inexplicable grace
                      unburdening my soul.

Her tiny body needful, yearning to be fed, guarded
With warmth, so dependent, so fragile
Yet to a spirit of colossal magnitude joined
That resonates away from here, gilded regions beyond,
Transcendent over time and constellation,
But emanating here, too, somehow at same time,
Coming to me in gentlest echo, sure and tranquil,
And stays with me in sweet re-echoing as she smiles
                           into my eyes.

Now watching over a backyard Kiera in a sandbox sits
On infinity's course, only for a brief time removed
From when she sat with angels on golden hillside
                       tracing heaven's wonders,
Where in purest light and goodness,
In spirit, substance, and workings ethereal
She was in God's sanctum basking.
Such very short time ago.

Her azure eyes afire glow translucent gem-crystals
Conduit to God's effulgent glory,
And who so seeing, being inwardly quickened,
And her luminous spirit of love feeling
As angelically she smiles,
And who now holding her, looking upon her, touched
By her ambrosial essence to the soul's renewal
                          and refreshing,
Can possibly the spirit of heaven not feel?
Or the existence and love of God deny?

2013

April

Adorable, Gift from the high realm of goodness
    Star-light brightest and warmest, angelic

    Name serenely soft like dewdrop on a daisy
    Smiles her Mom's smile.

Perfect, A twin
    Sister to brother Ollie

    Brings aura of autumn russet leaves light-raining
    Much missed and loved, Ollie same.

Radiant, Sunshine she gifts to every day
    Washington shower, shine, or mix

    Pink socks and fluffy dress mild-green and lacy
    Delicate, tiny feet pattering about.

Innocence-In her illuminated eyes
    Felt in her grandfather's heart as he held her

    By bond fifty-eight years bridged
    Over nine hundred miles he feels her pure sweetness.

Lovely, Peace of heaven aglow on her face
    Glee, love, and charm form star in her eyes

Like her Mom very stylishly hat-cute
Youngest granddaughter of mine.

April, A miracle
Born early autumn
Eternal joyous seasons.

2016

Giver of Voice

Some I heard were rid of their bodily afflictions by a Holy One
But forgot the curing Master, Purchaser of their pain and torment,
By no rendered gratitude in return for the intervention.

No day passes I do not see His calming countenance nor hear sound
of His sandals
As He walked upon the foreground in assured steady movement
Benignly, serenely, approaching me in His humble robe and tassels
And there blessed me, and stressed a greater gift called atonement.

Oh what words precious as gold-inscribed verse possibly can I utter
In burst of rejoicing hallelujah for the divine operation
Granting me voice to speak when for abundance of time prior
I lived helplessly agonizing without voice in dark desperation?

Oh what worthy, wondrous song possibly can I sing
In sweetest resounding praise of God's glorious and quickening spirit
Touching and mending my faculties for notes my voice to ring?

Above ground I stood upon, healed and awed by the Healer's power,
Hovered a watching bird whose empyrean song
Imbued the light, passing breeze as began the Giver's departure.
Feather song's echo faded to silence like sea wave to quiet ebb
While His footsteps on parting path purposed along.

There singing I cried out in thanks, all I could offer in gift to Him
The Master of my soul, Giver of my voice, Forgiver of my sin.

2015

Seed Everlasting

The seed of love
In rich soil embedded
Is better to hold the heart
And to grow
Than to be floating
Like a fanciful feather:
Of the moment a wisp of magic
Of fleeting sway,
Quickly to frail
Blows easily
Away.

What I so yearn
Is that seed to give you
Everlastingly,
That in sweetest fondness lies
And in pure love resides—
Birth to love's
Sublime-most harvests
Of the heart.

So the seed would thrive
By your soul touched,
To the fruit of being one—
Soaking in the rain
As if silvery showers
Of unutterable joy,
Then by the rainbow caressed.

Our souls the sun's rays
Breathing in
All the day long and for infinite days,
Ecstasy with wonder
As by angels we pass,
Our souls rising higher
Than ever we could aspire—
And even higher to
The celestial spheres.

2009

The Stallion-Hearted

There are the stallion-hearted who strive
Every day their all to deliver and ardently
                                        celebrate
Their verve to triumph, they're not merely
                                                alive.

Theirs are minds and hearts like iron stout,
They of spirit and will indomitable and immovable
                                                made
For battle, to silence the naysayer, vanquish any
                                                doubt.

All life's good, journey, and dreams as much for them
                                                as others,
Bliss and success as much for them to embrace
And they discover together a kinship, a mission,
                                        as brothers.

Life's fierce jouster in a rumbling, blazing onslaught at
                                                them
But they withstand, possessing a lion spirit and smart
                                                strategy
Dressed in Keller armor—resilience, drive, and courage
                                        their emblem.

They are as tough and determined as the others can be,
They are thoroughbreds of life, of a gallantry
                              great,
Having valor and unseen sources of strength, and souls
                                        as free.

2012

To the Highest Heights

I

At fifty-seven I race against Time with a gripping sense of urgency:
It's easy to relax, be lazy as my disease insists, so tempting
To stay tied to the couch and TV by the silken cords of ease.
But I have to exercise my body sufficiently
To make last as long as possible
The strength my body currently possesses.
I just have to force myself, fire up all fibers of my will
To work to avoid the dreaded chair by rowing a hand-trike,
As my oldest brother James bides time in a residential care center
There at the end of the uphill leg of my hand-trike route.

My hand-trike rolls, and to be rolling I row, working and sweating
to row.
Once moving, and moving further some, I gain momentum within
And after I row and roll by the place where James is
The resolve to see the workout to its end surges within me
As I then reach the route's downhill leg, which I rush down
In ecstasy and freedom and fulfillment of speed
That I produced by the power and sweat of my exertion.
And going downhill I soar

Soar even higher and as free as the gull gliding overhead
As I discover in the moment too I do this not by myself
Nor for just myself but somehow in unison with James
Being inspired by him, and even in the face of some wind flurry
Or uphill climb I can almost hear his voice on the stiff breeze

Whispering, "Brent, you can do this. You're strong enough.
You are getting stronger. Keep on going. Just keep on rowing."

James, in a state of a mere outer shell, a slight shadow
Of who he is, so I don't think he, primarily, lies in that bed:
Rather, his being with place here and place beyond
And the more in the beyond, I believe, and somewhere
In that balance of spirit, time and season he watches me rowing
And wheeling by, his spirit cheering and pushing me forward,
Onward, upward, his spirit-wind at my back.

II

On an early spring day fittest for conquering heights
The bar rose gradually in evenly-spaced notches marking inches
Of the elevations to which some jumped and where some faltered,
As competitors in number shrank, the vanquished having leaped as high
As their might, technique and upward thrust could vault them
Only to fall victim to the disdain of gravity.
The attempts of all the high school competitors but one
Each in turn to power and curve his body over the bar
Clipped the bar enough to jostle it off, some feeling it graze their bodies
In accompanying descent to the padded landing below.

One remained having survived, one lean, tall, and athletic
Named Clair, with his turn now, a chance to solely claim
The victor's crown if he cleared the bar.
So about to begin the attempt to master one last height
He stood at top of the take-off run area, preparing,
Eyeing the high jump bar and circulating directions throughout his body,
Through his mind running the sequence of essential movements
For his body to perform, and from the sheer force of concentration
Trying to transmit into his muscles extra capacity and energy
From the unspent reserves of power and strength within his body,
When he felt the caressing arm of one smaller than he around his back
And heard the one's voice declare affirmatively, reassuringly,
"Clair, I know you can clear that bar"—

The words those of his loyal, oldest brother James
Who had watched Clair's every successful jump
Leading up to this one he was to attempt.
The steel-sure, ascendant words washed over Clair,
Instantly his determination reinforced, his purpose heightened.
James then stepped back to the side expecting Clair's victory.
Such certainty not from the source of his own experience
For he could not have known the formula and exertion
For his younger brother to reach such winning height.
He never knew nor was capable of such physical prowess
For from birth had he been afflicted by a debilitating palsy.
But there undaunted stood James, waxing valiant
In his devoted allegiance and advocacy for Clair.

Off Clair bounded, striding gazelle-like on a semi-arc path
To the spot in front of the high jump standard
Where his bent left leg pushed up hard off the ground
Springing up his body in rhythm with his swung-upward arms,
right leg leading,
Catapulting himself up high, and just higher to bar level,
Then turning his legs and upper body square, followed by
The backward drive and curve of his shoulders, torso, and legs
In clean curl over the bar, and victory was his
And the victory as much James', who let out a jubilant euphoric roar
Setting off their glowing celebration that their brother-tie and fused wills
Produced a synergism that barely a moment before yielded the power
That propelled Clair over that bar, carrying James along with him.

III

James' body too long by disease vexed, emaciated, and worn:
Physically nigh unto death, reduced to a fragile frame
Now merely encasing his flesh and corporeality
And a ravaged, feeble mind forced upon him too early.
Yet his heart still at work as his undaunted lion spirit
Of Mt. Everest scale, child-pure and Job-refined,
In an unseen realm of Time and consciousness waits—

Certain of release soon from the chains of mortal burden
And assured of the verity of imminent transport
To a glory infinitely more than any
That a warrior, star-athlete, or honored gladiator
Could in victory or as hailed legend enjoy.

James very soon will clear the mortal bar
And rise in transfiguring ascendance, destined
To the highest heights scaled and reached
By those of God's children who were exemplary good
And who righteously endured despite severe adversity,
James undeniably the embodiment of both.
As upwardly he passes the jeweled portal to God's royal palace
Cheers will thunder forth for him from legions
Of angels and saints along the radiant marbled way.

Upon God's mountain James will see Jesus
And then from Him receive richest reward
For all his purity and goodness, his God-ward obedience
                                                              and love,
For all his Christ-likeness, and all his words and acts
That touched others, lifted them heavenward.
In perfect frame, in zenith joy, in perfect freedom
And upon the hills of glory he will move about
At the speed of a thought or desire that he wills.
He will command height, element, and distance.
For all Time, in the Hall of Fame of Righteous Souls,
In the elevated echelons of eternal paradise and tranquility,
It will of James be recorded and celebrated:
"He persevered! He conquered! He is champion!
He is truly free! He soars!"

James' brother #3
2014

Root Beer and Watermelon

In blazing summer, Lyle
A high school chemistry teacher,
Prepared with as much care and purpose
As that he earnestly applied
Tending his needful garden rows
Or fine-tuning a chemistry lesson,
For the scattered arrival throughout the sunny day
Of the drove of his grandchildren coming to visit,
Filling a gunny sack or two to the full
With juiciest watermelon and bottles of soda,

Then placing the heavy sacks in the side-yard ditch
Of water running cold as a mountain stream—
To us kids may as well have been
A magical underground well bursting forth
A fountain of root beer, Grape Nehi, and Orange Crush.
He knew all us kids would be hot and thirsty
By the time of arriving there
And some would have come in station wagons
Without air conditioning, so he knew
We'd love something refreshing and cool.

Grandpa's special formula of watermelon bust +
Root beer + Grape Nehi + Orange Crush +
His corny jokes sparking our laughter anyway
Synthesized our close bonds of joy with him.
For us wanting all the best, he loved seeing us
Happy with him, smiling and having fun—

He spitting out watermelon seeds
To the grass as we spat them out, and all of us
Laughing to abandon until our bellies ached.

Alongside the side yard of Lyle's home
Coursed the irrigation ditch, way-along
Its waters diverted at networked points
To gardens throughout the small town
By townsfolk planted and nurtured.
In brief season the vitalizing water to the garden plots
                                    quickened and grew them;
Grandpa Lyle's simple acts of love performed
        moved and enriched us for seasons lasting more,
And four generations along our grandchildren feel
Of Lyle's loving spirit and generous, kind heart
From our acts of sharing, care, and love
He taught us to give.

2015

Timeless Painting

Faculties for painting
Slipped from Miral years ago,
His brush stilled for a time
But not before he saw and portrayed
A lighthouse and a menacing shore cliff
And against it a violent thrashing
Of wind-whipped, frenzied waves,
And an old wooden ship off-shore in woes of sea
With its rigging and tattered masts
And long narrow posts and poles atremble
Straining from bow to stern, fighting
To withstand the ravages of the dusk storm
Before the darkness spreads its shroud
Over a sunset's late-lingering
And gradually-vanishing grayish-pink sky.

On hallway wall the painting has hung
Just outside small doorway of apartment
Of the artist Miral and his sweetheart.
A neighbor two doors down
Strolls through the hallway often,
Each time on his way by
Pausing to inspect the painting,
And mesmerized deeply into it asks
"What's to become of the beleaguered ship
In the just off-shore waters
In which it's floundering?"
"Will the lighthouse beacon and guide

Bring to safety of shore and shelter of home
The beset and distraught forlorn sailors
If any there be surviving?"

Masterpiece that belongs in a museum
Of fine works, precious gift from Miral
Who could not have foreseen
Many years later a hallway stroller
Stopping to gaze at his labor of love
That would live on and triumph over the fetters
Of mortal nature staying his brush and gift,
And would stimulate and stir the pen
Of the eye-sated and soul-touched stroller
Who pictures himself an artist

Creating and painting with words,
And oh hopes that his poetry
Will be of impact transcendent
Beyond his mortal constraints, beyond
The horizon of his mortal sojourn, and be
As gripping and breathtaking
And as timeless
As an intrepid ship, a fevered bruised sky,
An unruly sea, a forbidding cliff—

And a rescuing lighthouse.

2016
Dedicated to Miral and Doreen Thornton

Did You See

Did you last evening
See the sunset?
That sweep of radiance
There by nature's brushstroke
Did you behold
Before the hourglass of dusk
Drained the last few minutes
                         and seconds
Of sand and signaled
The dark sheet of night
Shrouding all?

Daylight shrinking
There was dark rose and orange-red,
Scarlet shades and
Crimsons hues teeming as though
In the sky's inner sanctum
The ether's full spectrum of orange to red
To purple combustion-like collapsed in on itself
Then burst outward, spraying empurpled strands
And those of varied reds—intermingled
And interwoven in a band of sky,
Like an invisible side geyser
Shooting in crimson, pink, and maroon some
To the western sky, and there
Caught and held in still-pose, motionless,
By the hand of the Supreme Author
                         of all creations,

Held festively fiery between
The dark rim beneath it
And the huddle above it
Of dark gray swelling clouds
In the darkening sky.

Not a blend or scheme
Or array of color
That on palette
An artist could finesse.
It's tapestry, symphony
And theater of color
That only God creates
Upon the firmament,
His canvas.

Did you see the two birds
                    (they may have been eagles)
Parallel and synchronized
Speed through the sky-scape
Inside the borders
Of the resplendent
As if right on script?
Astounding to your eyes
And mesmerizing
Your soul, too?

After the birds like lasers
Had sped out of view,
After the glorious glow
Into black vanished,
Into a state of wonderment I fell
Absorbing it all within
And could only feel
                    to celebrate

The designs and works
Of the Divine.

On the First Day
"Let there light," He said
And He set the day and night.
On the Fifth Day
He made the creature to fly
                    on a set of wings
Named it fowl
And called its home the skies.
And infinite evenings
Of woman and man
The sunset He has arranged
Just so, and so right,
So right for us;
And invited
The eagles to take part
And us to behold.

2010

Love Tale True

Town Monroe where two souls rose to blossom
And way embarked to ever one become
Like blissful song on zenith's wings carried
To where love-rapt souls wish to long tarry.

Town Monroe where they grew up and were reared
In a severe time that tried souls, flamed fears,
But hard work, faith and dreams the battle won
As town hopes broke from the dark to the sun
And of its grown-up young came these rare two—
A pianist and a star of the hoops.
Cupid divined the globe for such a pair
Poised arrow, released potion through sparked air.
The nectar of sweethearts in their blood ran,
"Forever and ever"—their tender plan.

He answered the call to a distant land
But first in marriage they joined their hands
With hearts in solemnity to God bound,
Then he departed. And long the time plowed.
Their first child they lost, he at three days old,
Though an ocean apart, they braved that cold;
God buoyed them up, secured their passage through
The dark clouds, onto path to the sky blue.
Three years in all, like an eternity
But grew their love in path of destiny.

Seven more children they brought to this life.
A gift priceless to bestow at time right
To their last child, like gold to impart:
His first name's first part, her first name's last part
And by the parts joined the daughter's name formed
To crown the blessing of all fruit they bore.

They gathered family around for meals.
To give thanks, seek God's blessing, the nine kneeled.
After prayer, around the table they sat
For mother's gourmet and a round of chat.
Ill word about the food, if one was bold,
Was also unwise for it drew dad's swift scold—
Slightest disrespect for his queen he'd crush
For unceasingly she'd toil for us.
Praise he rained on her sweet as the dessert
Then he rose from his chair to where stood her.
Suave as Cary Grant he played romantic,
Not outdone she worked her charm and magic.
Quite the spectacle as they hugged and kissed
And many times waltzed to the song of bliss.
Thus he honored his queen and she her king,
Celebrating their joy with their offspring.
Then they'd float away to wash the dishes
And the two talked, laughed, and shared their wishes.

When for twenty-six years they've been married
They're basking in love still, their love cherished
The evening he strides onto a dance floor
Surprising her. She's renewed to her core
At first sight of him, in their souls' heaven
Where they basked in Nineteen Forty-Seven.
Chemistry aflame in their eyes' gaze
Rendered to each other, they wordless praised
Renewal of their sweet oneness again:

Sparkling, electric, melodious blend.
One could see it in their illumined eyes,
Hear it in their voices, from their goodbyes.

Through the years they held a running debate
Whether in heaven basketball is played.
She thought the notion just too much folly,
Not a fan at all, her reading hobby
She enjoyed on the front row as he watched
The game unfolding, in the drama caught,
But she paid no mind despite all the noise;
For him the scoreboard, her—those words Tolstoy's.
He who had once a high school team coached,
She to whom a library was the most.
Once a local star who garnered some clips
Now on basketball's destiny his quips
Kidding her, but to her ridiculous
She would just reply, playful, "Oh, Carlos."

The other came first in every breath,
The constant of their love guiding their quest.
No matter the parched drought or coldest blast
Strong and serene they, held in their bond's clasp.
Whether living in a cramped apartment
Or comfort, they were happily content.
However the tide, season, or cadence
Of their linked lives, wherever their havens,
Just with each other, each other's presence,
Soared the mate to the highest resonance.
Simple times best like a round-the-block walk
Or in the kitchen in end-of-day talk;
Once so poor just carrot sticks they could take
To eat like candy on a movie date.
Then one day more prospered they hand-in-hand
On a Laie beach strolled midst the sand.

Hand-in-hand they oft walked through temple halls,
Their love's blessed destiny caught on mirrored walls.
His last mortal words that he spoke to her
Calm and poignant, spoken to reassure:
"Colleen, do you know how much I love you?"
He left before he could say, but she knew.
Inseparable, in steel-weld, their souls,
Impervious to withering, the cold;
Theirs a flame of love no unleashed power,
Force, element, or test can devour.
The last sojourn of her life pained and tried,
Ten years apart, and nights alone she cried
But she could feel near when she'd pass the Gate
To beyond, first to him, to his embrace.

On a sunny Sabbath early June day
His presence upon air stirred and weighed
And like light breeze upon a tiny leaf
There amid backyard quiet stayed her grief;
Seemed to surround the small ornate garden
And patio where she sat with a son.
For a moment he was there, they knew sure,
Tending to them, real as times she'd capture
Clear view of him from the kitchen window
Watching him cultivate a garden row.

Day of their new dawn, day of reunion
Came. She traversed, then he called her to come.
As the Gate opened their eyes fervent met,
And smiling they converged, and sweet tears shed;
They caressed each other with all soul's might
And their lips touched under heaven's pure bright.
They rejoiced and began singing so bold
The angels chimed in, and the chorus echoed:

"So let's tell the world
Of our new love divine,
Forever and ever
You'll be mine." [2]

They were not wealthy by mortal measures
But now partake of all of love's treasures.
Town Monroe where the two are laid to rest
Side-by-side, rib-to-rib, words in stone etched
Of tribute, of monument to their love,
Their romance, for heirs to take witness of—
A tale of love true in writ and song rings
Of Carlos and Colleen, on timeless wings.

Brent Asay
Son #4
2011

---

[2] "Forever and Ever" lyrics © Universal Music Publishing Group, EMI Music
Publishing

About the Author

The life journey of Brent Asay began on an early-summer day in Long Beach, California, in 1957. Through the ensuing fifty-nine years, he has lived in Utah, Texas, Hawaii, Japan, and Idaho. He claims that in the 1960s, he grew up in the best neighborhood on the face of the earth—Wilford Avenue in Murray, Utah. He is a firm believer in God, family, and church. He grew up in a family of ten and is the proud father of three children, and has seven wonderful grandchildren, with whom he loves to spend time, including Frisbee-tossing with his grandsons. Currently, he works and resides in Salt Lake City, Utah. When not working, he likes music, following politics, sports, reading, leisure travel as his circumstances allow, and of course, poetry. During the warm months, he enjoys getting out on his hand-trike.

CPSIA information can be obtained
at www.ICGtesting.com
Printed in the USA
FSHW020705010219
55409FS

9 781643 490328